Religion and Ethics

Ethics

Religion and Ethics

Ethics
for AS students
by Noel A Davies
Series Editor: Roger J Owen

C000090282

Acknowledgements

I am grateful for the opportunity to write about Religion and Ethics at a time when ethical issues raise challenging questions for religion. I owe a debt of gratitude to many people who have contributed directly or indirectly to the preparation of this book:

- to Trinity College, Carmarthen for first suggesting that I teach a course on Contemporary Ethics to undergraduate students;

- to the WJEC for their invitation to be an examiner in Religion and Ethics at A2 and AS level;

- to Roger Owen (Series Editor) and Cathy Grove (of UWIC Press) for their advice, expertise and support;

- those who are familiar with the literature in this field will recognize that I have been heavily dependent on the work of other authors in this field; every effort has been made to acknowledge these sources.

Above all, as always, I am grateful to Pat, my wife, for giving me 'space' to write this book and for her love, friendship and constant encouragement.

Noel A. Davies

Roger J. Owen, Series Editor

Roger J. Owen was Head of RE in a variety of schools for thirty years, as well as being a Head of Faculty, advisory teacher for primary and secondary RE, Section 23 Inspector and 'O' Level and GCSE Chief Examiner. Author of seventeen educational titles, he is currently an education consultant and WJEC Religious Studies AS and A2 Chair of Examiners.

Credits

Mark de Fraeye/Science Photo Library: cover, p. 70; Cathy Grove: p. 2(l), 12(l), 15(t,l), 16(l); The Photolibrary Wales: p. 2(t,r); Barbara Connell: p. 2(b,r); Capture Photography: p. 5(l), 12(r), 13(l and c), 15(b,l and c), 16(r); Geraint Wyn Jones: p. 5(c); Tegwyn Roberts: p. 5(r); Mary Evans Picture Library: p. 9, 11, 21, 24; Wendy Lawson: p. 10(l); Brian Brake/Science Photo Library: p. 10(r): Andy Dark: p. 12(c), 22; S. Scott-Hunter/Photofusion: p. 13(r); Wales Tourist Board: p. 14; Paul Doyle/Photofusion: p. 15(r); Mauro Fermariello/Science Photo Library: p. 17; David Fairfield/Getty Images: p. 18(l); Detlev van Ravenswaay/Science Photo Library: p. 18(r); Steve Casimiro/Getty Images: p. 32(l); Ghislain and Marie David de Lossy/Getty Images: p. 32(c); Omni Productions Ltd: p. 32(r); Wendy Dossett: p. 40; Andy Weber: p. 42; Rublev, Andrei (1360-c.1430), Icon with the Trinity, Moscow, Tretyakov State Gallery©SCALA, Florence, 1990: p. 46; Burstein Collection/Corbis: p. 52; World Religions Photo Library (www.worldreligions.co.uk): p. 53, 57, 59, 67, 68, 91(l); Swansea Hebrew Congregation: p. 61; Michael Marchant/Photofusion: p. 62; Brenda Prince/Photofusion: p. 63; Bob Krist/Corbis: p. 91(c); Stephen A. Land (with thanks to Karl and Lisa Jones and the Reverend Graham Canham): p. 91(r); The Info Group: p. 97; Crispin Hughes/Photofusion: p. 99; David Montford/Photofusion: p. 101.

Cover picture: The lotus, a significant symbol to Sikhs, Hindus and Buddhists (see p. 70).

Published by UWIC Press
UWIC, Cyncoed Road,
Cardiff CF23 6XD
cgrove@uwic.ac.uk
029 2041 6515
ISBN 1-902724-67-4

Design by *the info group*
Picture research by *Gwenda Lloyd Wallace*
Printed by *HSW*

Commissioned with the financial assistance of Awdurdod Cymwysterau, Cwricwlwm ac Asesu Cymru / the Qualifications, Curriculum and Assessment Authority for Wales (ACCAC).

Religion and
Ethics
for AS students
by Noel A Davies
Series Editor: Roger J Owen

Contents

Religion and Ethics

Introduction

This book does not assume any prior knowledge or experience of the ways in which religion and ethics interact with and inform each other. It presents material to meet the requirements of the WJEC AS specification; however, it should not be used as the only textbook for the Introduction to Religion and Ethics course, since advanced study requires the skills of wide reading and the analysis of a range of scholarly views on the issues being studied.

The book is designed to be used in tandem with the teachers' book, which provides more detailed background information on some of the topics covered and assistance with the tasks that appear in the text.

AS level candidates are expected to demonstrate not only knowledge and understanding, but also certain skills, such as the ability to sustain a critical line of argument, to justify a point of view, and to relate elements of their course of study to their broader context, as well as to specified aspects of human experience. Some of the tasks that appear below are designed to assist in developing these skills. Teachers and students will no doubt think of others.

This book, and the accompanying teachers' book, is constructed with Key Skills in mind. Students are asked to develop communication skills by taking part in discussions, gathering information and writing. They are asked to develop ICT skills through critically aware use of the Internet and are expected to present findings in the form of project dossiers and class presentations. They are asked to solve problems through making cases for particular viewpoints, and to work with others on joint research projects.

At the end of each chapter there is a short Glossary of terms. These are not intended to be exhaustive but offer brief definitions of terms that are not otherwise defined within the text itself. These should be used in tandem with the Glossary of Key Terms provided by WJEC.

Furthermore, in a subject such as Religion and Ethics it is not enough merely to learn specific facts, for example, about ethical theories or the ethical precepts of a world religion. The heart of the course is the development of skills of application and analysis. It is not enough to ask: 'What does this ethical principle mean?' Students will need to be asking throughout this course: 'How does this ethical principle help me to make an ethical decision about this particular issue?' The most important aspect of the course lies in discovering the ways in which the ethical principles in Section I can be applied to the topics of sexual ethics that are explored in Section II.

It is clear, therefore, that this course makes considerable analytical demands on students. It calls for the ability to explore three ethical theories, the ethical precepts of one major world religion and three topics of sexual ethics. In particular, it asks that the relationships between the ethical theories, the major world religion and the three topics should be studied with some care. With this in mind, Summary Charts are provided in the text. It cannot be over-emphasised that these do no more than present, in an easily understood format, a very basic, simplified outline of the key issues involved. They are not adequate in themselves. They are intended to aid study and revision but not to be the sole basis for study and revision. Students also need to recognise that very brief summaries such as these often over-simplify; they will, therefore, need to study the main text with some care but also to explore other resources in religion and ethics - including the Internet, which is a rich source of ethical debate as well as of stories that present contemporary ethical dilemmas relevant to this course.

Religion and Ethics for AS level students is a challenging course in that there are no easy answers to today's ethical questions. This book does not set out to provide students with the right answers, which they are then required to memorise. Rather it presents the tools that are required to enable students to make informed judgements and reach sustainable personal viewpoints on the topics presented. This requires students and teachers to be aware of the range of views that are possible, to explore them in a non-judgemental way and to present them in a succinct and clearly argued form. The WJEC examination will test this ability to present coherently more than one point of view in relation to an ethical issue or moral principle.

This book is offered as a resource in the challenging and fascinating task of confronting some of the most crucial questions facing our contemporary society.

Note about terms

Although there have been many debates among philosophers and ethical theorists about the difference between 'ethics' and 'morality', 'ethical' and 'moral', this book will assume that they mean the same thing and readers should not attempt to look for differences in meaning in the way these terms are used in subsequent chapters.

This book uses the abbreviations CE and BCE for Common Era and Before the Common Era. Some books use AD (Anno Domini) for CE and BC (Before Christ) for BCE. The actual years are the same, only the tag is different.

Aim of the section

After an introductory chapter which explores the nature and purpose of ethics and the relationships between religion and ethics, Section 1 will enable you to become familiar with the propositions of the three ethical theories which are set out in the Specification: Natural Law, Utilitarianism, and Situation Ethics.

You will be encouraged to evaluate their strengths and weaknesses and to consider the compatibility of the attitudes and principles of these theories with the traditional morality of the six major world religions.

Chapters 2 - 4 have a common structure:

- the key aspects of the theory are outlined;
- their strengths and weaknesses are evaluated.

Chapter 5 sets out the fundamental ethical framework of the six world religions.

Chapter 6 looks at the compatibility of the three theories with the traditional ethical approaches of the six major religions.

Chapters 5 and 6 each contain summary diagrams. These do not say all that there is to be said. They are intended as revision guides only. They seek to guide you as you try to hold together the main moral precepts of a religion, and the relationship between the three ethical theories and the religion you are studying. These charts do not provide all the information you need - fuller information is provided in the text of each chapter.

The Nature of Ethics

Aim

After studying this chapter you should be able to discuss questions such as: what is the nature of ethics, what is its purpose, what kind of questions does ethics seek to answer, who has the authority to make ethical decisions, what contribution does religion make to making ethical decisions today?

Exploring these questions at this stage will provide a firm foundation for studying the moral theories and specific ethical issues raised in subsequent chapters.

The nature of ethics

The human race is unique in that it has the ability - an ability not available to any other life form on earth, as far as we can tell - to make moral decisions and to act in accordance with those decisions. The moral questions that face us vary greatly from period to period. The basic principles that have been the foundation for these decisions have changed substantially too and continue to change.

Today, ethical decisions are more complex than they ever have been and it has become much more difficult to reach general agreement on moral issues. It is an uncertain and complex period when people, nevertheless, continue to look for guidance and leadership in relation to their personal life and the life of their society and nation.

We shall start to think about these issues by asking a series of basic questions:

1. What is the purpose of ethics?

At its simplest, ethics tries to answer the question:
- **What should I do?**

This could mean considering another question:
- **What attitude should I take?**

Basic to these questions is a deeper and more difficult question:
- **What kind of person should I be?**

> **Class discussion**
>
> *Discuss these three questions and outline your preliminary responses to them.*

Behind these questions are even more fundamental questions, such as:

- **What is the difference between right and wrong?**

- **How can I decide between right and wrong, between a right act and a wrong act?**

- **Is it always easy for me to distinguish between what is right and what is wrong?**

These questions have been formulated in the singular. This suggests that ethics or morality is a personal matter for individuals, a question for me to decide. But behaviour is never that simple. What I do, my attitude, the kind of person I am affects other people: my family, my friends, my neighbours.

So three further questions may be asked:

- What should **we** do?

- What attitude should **we** take?

- What kind of people or community should **we** be?

Class discussion

Consider these questions and discuss how your answers have changed now that the questions are posed in the plural rather in the singular.

Once we ask these questions the nature of the discussion changes fundamentally. I can no longer ignore other people and think only about my own needs, priorities and ideals. I have to take other people's needs into consideration. Indeed, these questions can extend the moral task so that it becomes a task for the whole of society. In the face of a specific challenge or threat or problem what should be our attitude as a society?

It is clear, therefore, that the moral task is extremely complex. It includes:

- the individual,

- the family

- the neighbourhood,

- the nation,

- the international community.

2. What kind of issues does ethics consider?

Personal questions:
For example, should I have the right to take my own life, either because circumstances mean that I am at the end of my tether or because I want to escape from the grasp of a terminal illness that is bound to bring suffering that will be painful and rob me of my self-respect?

Questions about my relationship with others:
For example, should I be prepared to have sexual intercourse outside marriage? Are homosexual relationships morally acceptable? Is a little deception in the workplace acceptable provided it does not cause harm to anyone else and that it goes undetected? How should society behave towards people who abuse members of their own family within their own homes?

Questions about the wider society or nation:
What should the priorities of our health service be? How should the government behave towards people form other countries who want to come to live here? How should we respond to racism? How can we decide whether genetic engineering is morally acceptable, and in what circumstances?

International questions:
Can war of any kind be justified when the armaments that are available are so powerful and destructive? Can we justify an international situation that permits 80% of the world's wealth to be in the hands of 20% of the population? In view of the destruction of the ozone layer and the increase in the temperature of the earth and its environment, should the international community agree international laws that enforce a way of life which is likely to diminish the dangers?

Task

Research task	Search recent copies of newspapers to find stories that raise ethical issues. Categorise them under the following headings:
	• personal behaviour
	• our relationships with others
	• the life of our nation
	• the international situation

3. Who is authorised to make moral decisions?

Many answers are possible. Consider these two statements:

I alone have the power and right to make decisions about matters that relate to my own life.

But, as we have already seen, none of us lives as isolated a life as that. Most of us live in a complex network of relationships with others. So I could argue that no one has the right to make moral decisions about my life unless I share in the decision. Unless, of course, I am no longer in charge of my mental faculties: who has the right then? Who has the authority over my life then?

Moral authority lies with the central institutions of society.

Surely, it is the task of the local authority, or the local health trust, or central government to formulate appropriate policies in relation to difficult moral issues that face society. For example, how much money should be spent on welfare services and how much we should spend on health? We have elected our representatives etc. to make these decisions. But there could be a problem: what if we do not accept the decisions made? What moral rights do we have then?

Class discussion

Consider the statement: 'I alone have the power and right to make decisions about matters that relate to my own life.' What are the arguments for and against it?

4. On what basis do individuals and society make such decisions?

A number of answers to this question are possible too:

The Christian Churches

In the days when the majority in British society were Christians, people would look to the Christian churches for guidance and moral authority and would act, more or less, in accordance with that guidance. Now, however, with less than 9% of the population of Britain (including Wales) regularly attending Christian worship, do the churches have any Christian authority or influence? What authority do the churches have in matters of personal and national morality when only a small number of people attend worship?

Other religions

We now live in a multi-faith and multi-racial country, that is, a country where a number of religions are practised and where there are people of many races. This at least means that there is more than one moral point of view at work in our society. People of different religious views can be in conflict with each other in relation to some issues. But they can agree with each other in relation to other issues.

Secular foundations

Others would claim that there is no rational basis for religion any more. They will seek alternative ways of making moral decisions. Are there other foundations available to us and do they have moral authority in the twenty first century? For example,

- Is a political ideology an adequate foundation?

- Could an acceptable philosophical framework be developed?

- Is it enough to follow social or cultural norms or conventions?

That is, is it ever enough to ask: 'what is morally acceptable to the majority of people in our society?'

5. Are absolute positions on moral matters (i.e. ethical positions that apply to everyone in every situation) possible or acceptable in a post-religious society?

It could be argued that some acts are wrong under all circumstances, whatever their effects on others and whatever the cost to the person him or herself.

For example, Judaism and Christianity would want to argue that some (at least) of the Ten Commandments (which can be found in the Book of Exodus and the Book of Deuteronomy in the Bible or Hebrew Scriptures) are in this category. 'You shall not kill' and 'You shall not commit adultery' are absolute moral commandments in all situations. They completely forbid killing and adultery.

Others would want to understand these commandments, which appear to be absolute, in the light of the history of the Jewish nation in the Bible or Hebrew Scriptures. Cruel killing and conflict in the name of God are regular events as Israel takes possession of the land of Canaan, for example. Often, too, sexual intercourse outside the marriage relationship is accepted as part of the pattern of life; sometimes it is punished, sometimes it is accepted as an inevitable aspect of the pattern of belonging and loving.

Which is the right attitude? Do Jewish and Christian Scriptures teach an absolute morality or do they offer a much more uncertain moral teaching? These are difficult and confusing questions and many people who wish to base moral decisions on religious foundations will often find it difficult to decide which path to take.

Task

Research task	Search the literature about **one other major world religion** with a view to answering the question: Does this religion teach an absolute morality or does it have a more flexible and adaptable approach to ethical issues?

But if we reject these religious foundations, is moral absolutism still possible? Some philosophers have attempted to answer the questions 'What should I do?' on rational foundations without any reference to religious or theological categories. They would claim that **some things are necessary and absolute whatever the circumstances**.
Others would argue, of course, that to look for absolute moral principles is completely inappropriate in our day. This is the age of disintegration, an age when the old certainties have disappeared forever. We should not try to re-establish an age that has disappeared. We must live with the moral disintegration and the complex and confusing morality and teaching which are the inevitable consequences. In his book *The Ethics of Uncertainty*[1] John Elford argues that, in Western society and in an age of uncertainty, we should acknowledge that moral certainty is impossible and we should not attempt to avoid the consequences of having to live with uncertainty.

6. In the light of these explorations, what is the relationship between religion and ethics?

Roger J Owen[2] suggests three possible approaches as follows:

(a) Morality depends on religion

Since our reasoning ability and experiences differ remarkably, individuals can come to diametrically opposite ethical judgements. Reason and experience alone cannot provide a workable system of ethics because it cannot deal effectively with human prejudice and selfishness. A more objective and authoritative view is needed. If there is a God, then God by definition is the highest moral authority and is the ultimate source of moral judgement. So some religious believers will take statements about ethical issues found in their sacred writings as authoritative and applicable to all situations in every generation. Or they will accept as authoritative the ethical views held by their religious leaders. This is absolutist ethics.

(b) Morality and religion are interdependent

Ethics and religion depend on a common source for their principles and values. There is an almost universal sense of moral obligation and an intuition as to what is right and wrong that is compatible with religious ideals but may not be derived from religious ideas (such as not committing murder). There is a common awareness of awe and wonder, of the mystical, of spirituality and so on, that can be, but is not necessarily, religious. For example, whilst Aquinas clearly applied Natural Law principles (see chapter 2) as an expression of his belief in God, Aristotle argued for the same basic concepts without any religious perspectives.

(c) Religion and morality are independent

Moral responsibility requires personal freedom to make decisions rather than have them imposed by an authority, religious or otherwise. Ethical principles are based on reason and experience without reference to religious beliefs or concepts. Religion is based on an assumption: the existence of God. Moreover, different religions sometimes have conflicting ethical views of issues (e.g. the number of marriage partners to have at any one time). This is not to say that such ethical stances are anti-religion or that religious believers cannot adopt that ethical stance, merely that it is not based on prior religious ideas.

With this understanding of the nature of ethics in mind, the primary aim of the following chapters is to ask, within the limits of the AS Religion and Ethics course: how do we discover moral principles which are relevant at the beginning of the twenty first century? We will have to begin by going back to the beginning and asking: 'What are some of the traditional approaches to moral principles?'

Task

Writing tasks	'For far too long, morality has been supposed to be based on religion. Too often, religious teaching, for example, on heaven and hell, has been used by leaders in society to encourage the population as a whole to live moral lives.... In a multicultural society, we need to develop a secular morality - of equality, honesty, fairness - which can unify, rather than divide... Championing this secular morality requires confidence and bravery.' (Based on a leader article in *The Observer*, 9/9/01, in response to the Archbishop of Westminster's admission that Christianity is being "vanquished" from government and people's lives in Britain.)
	(a) Explain why some would claim that morality is impossible without religion.
	(b) 'Religious teaching on heaven and hell is essential to encourage the population as a whole to live moral lives.' Assess whether this claim is valid today.

Glossary

absolute morality/ moral absolutism	a moral or ethical position which is based on principles to which there can be no exception under any circumstances
objective view	a view which is not based on a personal opinion (the opposite of subjective)
philosophical framework	a pattern or structure of thought based on reason and logic
political ideology	the basis upon which people or nations develop political policies
rational	based on reason and logic
secular	a society in which religion no longer plays a central role in individual or community life
theological	based on a belief in a God

Natural Law

Aim

After studying this chapter you should be able to show clear understanding and knowledge of the moral principles of Natural Law.

This is a fundamental ethical theory because

- *it is one of the first attempts at establishing a framework for moral decision-making;*
- *Thomas Aquinas developed Natural Law as a basis for Christian morality;*
- *it has been widely used as a basis for Christian morality;*
- *it also provides a philosophical framework which is compatible with other world religions.*

You should also be able to explain your personal response to Natural Law and provide examples of the way in which it can be used to make moral decisions today.

ÉDUCATION D'ALEXANDRE PAR ARISTOTE

An engraving showing Aristotle, the Greek philosopher, tutoring Alexander the Great.

The beginnings: Aristotle

The beginnings of Natural Law can be traced back to the Greek philosopher, **Aristotle (384-322BCE)** and the Stoics (from the third to the second century BCE). Its basic principle is that:

- since everything has a purpose,

- since the natural world has a design, and

- since fulfilling that design is the greatest 'good'

therefore human reason can be used to explore and discover those moral principles that are inherent within the natural world and should be followed in order to fulfil the highest moral 'good'.

It is important to recognise that Natural Law as developed by Aristotle was based on a secular philosophy and did not depend on religion for its validity.

Seminar topic

Look at these pictures of natural beauty and natural disaster.

• **Describe your response to what you see.**

• **What is good about it?**

• **What is bad about it?**

• **Assess whether the three principles set out above are still valid today.**

Thomas Aquinas

Natural Law was further developed within a Christian framework by **Thomas Aquinas (1225-1274)**. St. Thomas was a Roman Catholic priest and theologian. He used this secular philosophy as a basis for Christian morality. He believed that it was possible to offer a 'rational' basis for Christian morality using 'Natural Law'. His claim was that morality did not necessarily depend on divine revelation, (that is, God being made known through God's own initiative, or through the Bible, or through the Church, for example). Human beings could discover what was morally good without any reference to these at all. Ever since, Natural Law has dominated Catholic morality and has had considerable influence on other Christian traditions. (Chapter 5 examines the compatibility of Natural Law with the six major world religions.)

Natural Law, as developed by Aquinas, can be summarised in terms of the following four characteristics:[3]

- For Thomas Aquinas **the foundation of Natural Law was his religious belief that God had created the world**, that God established within it an order and pattern and purpose which reflects God's will.

- If everything has been created for a purpose, **human reason, by reflecting on that purpose, can judge how to act** in order to conform to that purpose.

- In Natural Law **an act does not depend for its moral justification on the act's having any particular consequence** - unlike Utilitarianism, for example (see chapter 3). An act can be considered to be morally good in itself, even if it leads to suffering.

- Since Natural Law is based on reason rather than revelation, **it can be discerned - in theory - by anyone, whether or not they are religious**.

Thomas Aquinas, the Italian theologian, as represented in Butler's 'Lives of the Saints'.

Class discussion

Does belief in God or a transcendent being/beings make it easier or more difficult to accept the principle of Natural Law?

The four characteristics set out above suggest a number of questions:

1. What is the purpose of life?

Aristotle's answer to this question suggested that:

- **everything done by an individual or a group of individuals aims at some purpose or other**, whether good or evil. Nothing we do is without a purpose;

- **there are 'higher' and 'lower' aims**. We undertake an act with a lower aim in order to fulfil a higher aim. For example, we learn to use a computer (an act with a lower aim) in order to be able to write this book more effectively (a higher aim);

- **the ultimate aim, above all other aims, for an individual, a community of individuals or a nation, is to fulfil 'the highest good'**. Aristotle suggested that happiness is the best definition of this 'highest good';

- **a distinction should be drawn between an efficient cause and a final cause.** If I ask, 'Why did I break my leg?' I could answer in terms of 'efficient cause' and explain that I fell because I was carrying a heavy parcel, that there was ice on the path and that I did not see the step. But an answer in terms of 'final cause' could talk about God's purpose in 'allowing' me to fall, the lessons about the meaning of life that I have learned as a result of breaking my leg, and the importance of the experience in enabling me to deal with pain and vulnerability in a more positive way than before. 'Efficient cause' is about practical explanations; 'final cause' seeks to set out the ultimate meaning and purpose of an event;

Seminar topic

(a) Work in pairs to develop a definition of individual happiness.

(b) Share your definitions with the others in the class.

(c) 'The happiness of a community' or 'general happiness' should be a main goal for government policy. Discuss this claim.

- greater priority should be given to **the highest good** of a community or state than to the highest good of an individual:

'For even if the good of the community coincides with that of the individual, it is clearly a greater and more perfect thing to achieve and preserve that of a community; for while it is desirable to secure what is good in the case of an individual, to do so in the case of a people or a state is something finer and more sublime.'[4]

Thomas Aquinas developed this theory further. As a Christian theologian and philosopher, he believed that **for a Christian, God who created all things and gave everything its pattern and purpose, is the 'highest good'. God, therefore, is the goal and destiny of every human being, even if everyone does not acknowledge this.**

He believed also that every human being willed what is good, since every person has a human nature - created by God - that is common to all. This is an 'ideal' human nature to which each person can be true or of which they can fall short. Our moral acts are central in relation to this human nature.

Task

Writing task	(a)	How would you define individual happiness?
	(b)	Explain how you would understand the phrase 'the happiness of a community'.

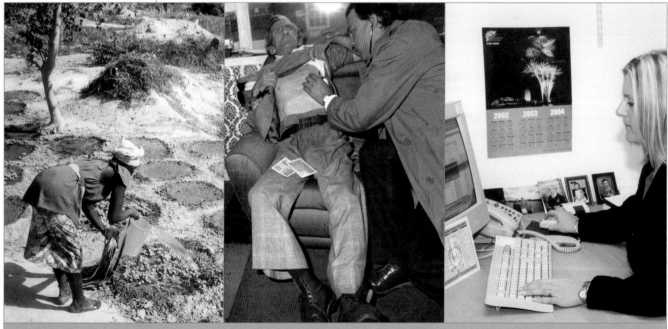

How would you describe what is going on in these pictures in terms of (a) higher and lower aims and (b) efficient and final cause?

What do these photographs tell you about the 'ideal' human nature and 'falling short' of the ideal human nature?

This brings us to sin! Sin is a key concept in Christian theology and ethics. **Aquinas defined sin as falling short of the good, being less than God intended us to be**, seeking false good rather than the truly good.

2.   How can we discover this highest good?

Aquinas' answer, following Aristotle, was: **through human reason**. The human nature given to human beings by God enables them to use their reason and experience to understand what is right. **The moral life, therefore, is life lived according to reason**.

Indeed, for Aquinas acting according to reason was the same as acting as a Christian, since acting according to reason did not conflict with the will of the God who created the world and gave to humankind the ideal human nature which is ours. He believed, therefore, that it was possible to understand the chief virtues that were the foundations of the moral life (patience, self-discipline, courage and justice, according to Aristotle) through reason alone.

This is the heart of Natural Law: using reason to discover the highest good that we should aim for. We have the ability to use reason to make intentional moral decisions, which Aquinas calls 'human acts', as opposed to instinctive acts. Of course, human reason must be used correctly. It can be used for evil purposes or for the greater good. Only the latter is, in Aquinas' terms, 'the right use of reason'.

So the key question is: does this act aim at achieving the highest good or not?

Seminar topic

How would you answer the question, 'What is the meaning of life?' How does your answer differ from that of Aquinas?

Task

Research task	Using Information Technology to explore issues of sexual ethics:

Research task   Using Information Technology to explore issues of sexual ethics:

(a)   Use the BBC Religion and Ethics website (http://news.bbc.co.uk) to identify up to three stories that raise issues of sexual ethics.

(b)   What are the ethical issues that are raised by these stories?

(c)   How would asking the question, 'Does this act aim at achieving the highest good?' help you to make moral decisions about these ethical issues?

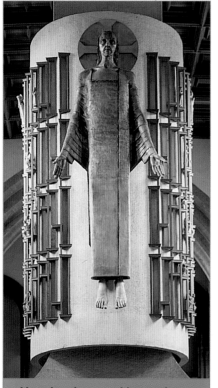

How does Jesus enable people today to understand and know God?

3. Is there a place for revelation?

Since Aquinas was a Christian theologian and philosopher, this was a key questions for him. Traditionally, Christians believe that through 'revelation' God makes God's self known in Jesus Christ, in the Bible and through the Church. We do not find God by searching; God is made known to us by God. According to one important tradition, **it is only through revelation that the will and purpose of God can be known**. That is, it is God who takes the first step by making known God's will and purpose (through the Holy Spirit, in Jesus Christ, in God's Word in the Bible and through the Church). Thus, it is totally dependent on what God chooses to do for us rather than on our rational powers. On this basis, Natural Law, the main moral philosophy of the Roman Catholic Church since the Middle Ages, was rejected by the Protestant Reformers of the 16th century (for example, Martin Luther and John Calvin) since Natural Law gave human beings a moral status which was independent of what God freely does for us.

However, although Aquinas does give priority to human reason he also insists that **it is possible to accept the principle of Natural Law while also believing in God's revelation**. God, who created the world, gave to humankind the one ideal human nature and gave us the ability to use our human reason. God has also revealed the being of God to us.

4. How can Natural Law be applied to particular moral issues?

This is done by applying 'casuistry'. Casuistry begins with the fundamental moral principles of Natural Law and applies them rationally to particular situations. There is a general tendency to be very critical of casuistry, which is often understood as an ability to justify any act provided a person is able to apply arguments with enough subtlety and cunning! However, this is to misinterpret casuistry at its best and there is a strong tradition of responsible casuistry that seeks to apply Natural Law to specific situations using human reason.

A number of examples can be given of ways in which Natural Law can be applied to particular issues. One of the key issues is sexual morality, an area in which Natural Law has been applied to moral decision-making, especially within Christian morality.

The argument can be set out as follows:

(i) According to Natural Law, the ultimate aim of the sexual act is to conceive a child.

(ii) Every other sexual experience must serve this purpose, whether or not we realise it.

(iii) Therefore, according to Natural Law, every sexual act that is not intended to conceive a child, or which could not lead to conception, is immoral.

(iv) Consequently, contraception, homosexuality and self-pleasure (masturbation etc.) are regarded as immoral since they cannot, by definition, serve the ultimate aim of sexual acts, namely, conceiving a child.

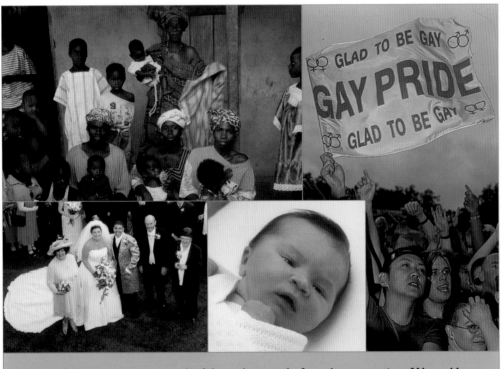

Write a short commentary on each of these photographs from the perspective of Natural Law.

(A traditional Christian version of this argument would add that Natural Law demands that sexual intercourse is morally acceptable only between husband and wife within marriage because:

• marriage is ordained by God for the union of man and woman (see Genesis 2: 24);

• the divine purpose of sexual intercourse is procreation;

• procreation or the transmission of human life is the central purpose of the marriage union;

• love and fidelity within marriage is essential for the proper bringing up and nurturing of children;

• Jesus' teaching reaffirms this understanding of marriage (see Matthew, 5: 27-32) and that any sexual intercourse outside marriage is morally unacceptable.)

Seminar topic

Discuss the following questions that arise from this argument:

• *On what grounds could it be argued that the only 'natural' purpose of sex is to conceive children?*

• *Explain why marriage is a 'natural' social and personal framework for sexual intercourse. Try to suggest what role religion played in the development of this understanding of marriage.*

Strengths of Natural Law

A number of strengths suggest themselves:

- The main strength of Natural Law is that it seeks to set out general ethical principles that are valid for everyone in all situations.

- Natural Law seeks to evaluate the inherent morality of an act (i.e. whether or not an act is ethical in itself) rather than seeking to decide its morality in terms of the consequences of the act.

- It avoids the danger of each person seeking to develop his or her own ethical stance to suit their own personal context and lifestyle. In this way it offers a firm and universal foundation for ethical decision-making.

- It has the advantage also of using our understanding of the natural world and the powers of human reason to develop ethical principles.

- Over the centuries Natural Law has become the philosophical basis for much religious thinking on ethical issues and is, therefore, deeply embedded within religious traditions such as the Catholic tradition.

Weaknesses of Natural Law

(a)   How do we decide what is natural?

If the laws of nature are used as our basis, our understanding of these laws changes as we know more and more about the natural world. Does this mean that the principles of Natural Law should change as human understanding and knowledge changes? If so, this could mean that the moral law would vary from culture to culture and between one period of human history and another. Does this not contradict the basic premise of Natural Law, namely, that it offers a moral framework that is common to everyone in all places and times, because we all share the same ideal human nature?

Does morality vary between different communities?

(b)   If the laws of nature (which reflect the design and purpose of the universe) are the basis of Natural Law, should not these laws be allowed to determine our actions?

Should a doctor have power over life and death?

For example, if a person appears to be terminally ill as a result of 'natural causes' is it morally appropriate, on the basis of Natural Law, to interfere medically in the natural progress of the disease or should the disease be allowed to take its natural course? And if a doctor does not make every effort to stop this natural progress and seek to prevent or delay death, is this not contrary to a doctor's moral responsibility to use all available medical treatments to save human life?

(c)   Is the premise of Natural Law (that there is an order and purpose and pattern in the natural world and in human nature) acceptable in the 21st century?

Many scientists - physicists and biologists, for example - would argue that chance rather than design or necessity determines the pattern of the chemical reactions that are the basis of natural life. Many would claim that it is no longer possible to talk about order and purpose - nor, some would claim, about a Creator - if we accept that accidental processes are behind the formation and continuation of the universe. In which case, the foundations of Natural Law crumble!

Chance or design?

(d)   It could be argued that Natural Law is in conflict with a Christian or religious ethic.

As we have seen, many Christian traditions argue that the Christian claim is that God has been revealed in a unique way in Jesus Christ, through the Bible and cannot be found by human reason. If this is true, does this not undermine the claim of Natural Law? Aquinas argued that the general principles of Natural Law do not clash with a Christian morality, rooted in revelation, because seeking the highest good is always to fulfil God's ultimate purpose for humankind.

Proportionalism

Sometimes Natural Law requires that the morally right act should be done even if it has bad consequences. Is it possible to justify a morally wrong act because it is likely to have good consequences? One way of achieving this is by proportionalism, which emerged from the Natural Law tradition and which Vardy and Grosch[5] define as the principle that holds 'that there are certain moral rules and it can never be right to go against these unless there is a proportionate reason which would justify it.'

For example, it could be argued that killing another human being is normally morally unacceptable. But in some situations, for example, during a painful terminal illness, it could also be argued that the demands of love towards the person who is suffering justify another person's helping to bring the life of the sufferer to an end, so avoiding any further terrible pain.

Tasks

Writing tasks

A group of religious and secular leaders has been invited to set out an agreed basis for contemporary ethics. They have decided to begin their discussions by considering Natural Law.

One person claims that Natural Law has been a basis for ethics for many centuries and that it has provided - especially in the concept of 'the highest good' - a tool by which people from different religions have been able to make ethical decisions. Another member of the group claims that without faith in God, Natural Law has no foundation and, therefore, could not be used as a basis for contemporary ethics, especially sexual ethics, in a society where the majority does not follow any religion.

(a)   Outline the main principles of Natural Law.

(b)   Determine whether Natural Law provides an adequate basis for sexual ethics today.

Chapter 2

Glossary

creator	God who has created the universe
instinctive acts	acts which human beings perform because it is their natural inclination, rather than because they have made a deliberate decision to act in a particular way
necessity	the belief that natural events and processes are the result of deliberate action and design by a transcendent being or are an inevitable result of the way in which the universe has been formed
ordained by God	given and ordered by God
Protestant	Churches that have their origins in the European Reformation, inaugurated in the sixteenth century by Luther, Calvin and Zwingli
Roman Catholic Church	a world wide Christian Church which has its origin in the very earliest period of Western Christianity, is focussed on the Pope, and has its centre in Vatican City in Rome
transcendent being	a being who is outside the realm of time and space which human beings occupy
world religions	religions that are practised by large proportions of the world's population; for the purposes of this book, these are Buddhism, Christianity, Hinduism, Islam, Judaism, and Sikhism

Utilitarianism

Aim

After studying this chapter, you should be able to show an understanding of the main principles of the theory of Utilitarianism as it was developed by Bentham and Mills, including the hedonic calculus and the two principles of act Utilitarianism and rule Utilitarianism.

You should also be able to apply the theory to contemporary situations that raise moral questions, weighing up the strengths and weaknesses of Utilitarianism.

The beginnings: Jeremy Bentham

The basis for Utilitarianism, as the name suggests, is **'utility'** (from the Latin, utilis, useful):

We should aim, in all situations where there is a moral choice, to act in such a way as to ensure the greatest happiness for the greatest number of people.

This is the heart of Utilitarianism: 'the greatest happiness for the greatest number.'

The theory of Utilitarianism was originally formulated by **Jeremy Bentham (1748-1832)**. Bentham was primarily motivated by his concern for the social conditions of his day rather than by a desire to formulate a moral theory as such. He believed that it would be possible to judge the good or evil in a particular action according to the consequences of the action:

'By utility is meant that property of any object, whereby it tends to produce benefit, advantage, pleasure, good or happiness, (all this in the present case comes to the same thing) or (what comes again to the same thing) to prevent the happening of mischief, pain, evil, or unhappiness to the party whose interest is considered: if that party be the community in general, then the happiness of the community: if a particular individual, then the happiness of that individual.'

(from an Introduction to the Principles of Morals and Legislation, 1789, chapter 1, section III)

A portrait of Jeremy Bentham, used on a business card of the period. Why do you think a French chocolate maker would use Bentham to promote his products?

Task

Research / Writing task	'Evaluating the benefit, advantage, pleasure, good or happiness of a person or community is an effective way of making moral decisions today.' (a) Produce a questionnaire that tries to discover answers to the following questions: • What do people mean by 'benefit, advantage, pleasure, good and happiness'? • How would they measure these characteristics? • Do they think that these are helpful in making moral decisions today? (b) Devise ways of testing your questionnaire within the school/college. (c) Use computer graphics to present your findings e.g. using a pie chart.

The Hedonic Calculus

Since 'happiness or pleasure' is so difficult to define and since these concepts vary so much from person to person and from situation to situation, Bentham suggested 'the hedonic calculus' as a means of defining happiness or pleasure. (Hedonic or Hedonism comes from the Greek word, hedone, which means happiness or pleasure). The Hedonic Calculus is the central principle of Utilitarianism.

In considering this principle the key questions are: What is happiness? How can 'the greatest happiness' be measured?

Bentham suggested seven criteria by which happiness or pain could be measured:

- **intensity**: is the happiness or pain deep or superficial?

- **duration**: is it temporary or more permanent?

- **certainty**: how sure are we that a particular act will lead to pain or happiness?

- **extent**: does the happiness or pain touch the whole life of a person or community or does it only affect limited aspects?

- **nearness (or propinquity)**: does the act create pain or happiness for people closely around us or for people far away from us?

- **richness (or fecundity)**: is it a happiness or a pain that enriches or impoverishes life (and not only in material terms)?

- **purity**: is the act morally pure or morally ambiguous?

Notice that the purpose of this hedonic calculus is to measure the moral value of a particular act by measuring the consequences of the act in terms of the quantity of happiness or pain rather than the quality. The emphasis here is not so much on the question: is this act good or evil in itself? But rather, the key question is: Are the consequences of this act good or evil?

This is the Consequentialist Principle: it is not the inherent morality of an act in itself that is fundamental, but rather the consequences of the act in the lives of individuals or communities. This principle is basic to Utilitarianism.

To summarise:

- Utilitarianism is based on utility or usefulness.

- The central concept of the theory is 'the greatest happiness for the greatest number'.

- Happiness (or its opposite, pain) can be measured using the hedonic calculus.

- The consequence of an act, not the quality of an act in itself, is the key to this principle.

Criticism

Bentham's theory and the hedonic calculus have been criticised for a number of reasons. Vardy and Grosch note three criticisms:

- Its basis is to measure happiness in terms of quantity rather than quality. But is it possible to evaluate happiness solely in terms of quantity, rather than on the basis of the nature and quality of the happiness experienced by a person or persons?

- The principle is entirely dependent on the possibility of being able to predict the consequences of any act. But is it always possible to predict with any certainty what the consequences of a particular act will be? And how is it possible to make

Seminar topic

How would you defend divorce on the basis of Utilitarianism?

How would you oppose divorce on the basis of Utilitarianism?

moral decisions in relation to acts that could lead to both pleasure and pain?

- **It is difficult to define what should be counted as pleasure and what should be counted as pain**. It may be that a person may be prepared to endure some physical, mental or emotional pain in order to experience a greater happiness. It may be also that what will be a pleasurable consequence for me would be a painful consequence for you!

Class discussion

Are these fair criticisms of Bentham's theory of Utilitarianism?

A new emphasis: John Stuart Mill

John Stuart Mill (1806 – 1873) realised that these questions were raised by Bentham's understanding of Utilitarianism and so was anxious to re-interpret Bentham's theory:

- He emphasised the quality of happiness or pain rather than its quantity or extent. He tried to distinguish between higher pleasures (which enjoy 'a superiority in quality' and which are associated with the mind) and lower (or inferior) pleasures that are associated with the body. Clearly these cannot be entirely distinguished from each other, but when the needs of the body (for example, for food and warmth) have been met then it would be possible to concentrate on seeking to attain the higher moral goals such as the intellectual, the cultural and spiritual.

- He called for a morality that was based not so much on what is desirable but on what is good and beneficial - such as truth, beauty, love and friendship. He was realistic about human nature and realised that people generally sought to satisfy the inferior pleasures rather than the superior pleasures, but he did not believe that this weakened in any way his emphasis on the greater moral worth of the superior pleasures:

A caricature of J S Mill by the cartoonist 'Spy' in Vanity Fair magazine 1873.

> 'Capacity for nobler feelings is in most natures a very tender plant, easily killed, not only by hostile influences, but by mere want of sustenance... (People) lose their high aspirations as they lose their intellectual tastes, because they have not time or opportunity for indulging them; and they addict themselves to inferior pleasures, not because they deliberately prefer them, but because they are either the only ones to which they have access or the only ones which they are any longer capable of enjoying...'[6]

- He sought to relate Utilitarianism more closely to the Christian ethic ('loving your neighbour as yourself constitutes "the ideal perfection of utilitarian morality" ')[7]

> 'The utilitarian morality does recognise in human beings the power of sacrificing their own greatest good for the good of others, It only refuses to admit that the sacrifice is itself a good. A sacrifice that does not increase or tend to increase the sum total of happiness, it considers as wasted.'
>
> (ibid.)

- He believed that rules had a positive contribution to make within a utilitarian ethic. For example, society needs the rule that states that people should tell the truth and that no one should benefit from telling lies. This rule (that human beings should always speak the truth) ensures the greatest happiness for the greatest number. Breaking this rule would in the long term lead to a decrease in the sum total of happiness.

Criticism

Although Mill tried to respond to aspects of the criticism of Bentham's utilitarian ethic, some problems remain. Vardy and Grosch note two criticisms:

- **How is it possible to distinguish between higher pleasures and lower pleasures?** How is it possible to make distinctions among higher pleasures? For example, is the pleasure of reading a play by, say, Shakespeare or Harold Pinter, of the same quality as playing soccer or hockey for the Welsh team? And how can this be decided? As Henry Sidgwick (1838-1900) commented: if all superior pleasures are of equal quality it makes no difference which we choose!

- **Is it possible to rely on a moral theory that is based on a single moral principle, namely, the greatest happiness of the greatest number?**

'Life's ethical dilemmas cannot be reduced to a pre-packaged, predictive calculus that balance outcomes. We experience internal conflicts between what our reason tells us, what duties we feel we ought to perform, and the need, obviously, to bring about the greatest good.'[8]

Class discussion

Is the principle of "the greatest happiness for the greatest number" still valid in the 21st century?

Versions of Utilitarianism

Attempts have been made to define different kinds of Utilitarianism, based on the work of Bentham and Mills. Two primary forms can be identified:

1.   Act Utilitarianism

This version begins by asking which act or acts lead to the greatest happiness for the greatest number and then, on the basis of these responses, tries to create general moral laws. Some have attempted to make this principle more workable by using the term 'sufficient happiness' rather than 'greatest happiness'.

2.   Rule Utilitarianism

This version begins by trying to agree on general moral rules and proceeds to devise specific acts which are morally acceptable or unacceptable on the basis of these rules.

In comparing these two versions of Utilitarianism it can be seen that:

(a)   *act Utilitarianism* begins with actions in order to develop ethical rules, while *rule Utilitarianism* develops rules in order to agree on morally acceptable action.

(b)   *act Utilitarianism* places the greatest emphasis on the consequences of a particular action. The danger here is to consider an action to be morally right provided the consequences are good, whether or not the motives for the action are good and just or not. Can morally acceptable consequences justify an action that is essentially immoral? For example, was plotting to assassinate Hitler during the Second World War morally acceptable, because its likely consequences (namely, putting an end to Nazism and its horrific policies) justified an essentially immoral act (namely, killing another person)?

On the other hand, rule Utilitarianism seeks to define what is morally right by considering the consequence of acting on the basis of particular rules, rules which are based, of course, on the principles of Utilitarianism. (For example, if the moral rule is to seek the well-being of the majority is it acceptable to seek the economic well-being of the majority in Wales if that means adopting economic policies that are likely to be detrimental to the majority in the world's poorest countries?) One of the attractive aspects of rule Utilitarianism is that it does at least allow moral rules, which can ensure equal rights.

There has been debate among scholars about whether John Stuart Mill was an act Utilitarian or a rule Utilitarian. Mel Thompson claims that Mill was the one who put forward rule Utilitarianism ('the rather more sophisticated approach') on the grounds that rules developed on the basis of utilitarian principles should be respected as being 'for the benefit of society as a whole.'[9] On the other hand, Vardy and Grosch describe both Bentham and Mill as act Utilitarians, because they seek to define what is ethically right in terms of the consequences of a particular action.

It is not easy to resolve this difference of opinion, but the following quotations from Mill's work may throw some light on the debate. At one point[10] Mill refers to the conception of happiness or utility - which is the basis of Utilitarianism - as 'the directive rule of human conduct'. Similarly, Mill describes the Greatest Happiness Principle as

> '...the end (i.e. purpose) of human action... (and) the standard of morality which may accordingly be defined (as) the rules and precepts for human conduct, by the observance of which an existence (exempt as far as possible from pain, and as rich as possible in enjoyments, both in point of quantity and quality)... might be... secured to all (hu)mankind...'

These quotations seem to indicate that for Mill the conception of greatest happiness (or higher or superior pleasure) for the greatest number was in itself a rule and a standard for moral behaviour.

More recently another form of Utilitarianism, namely **preference Utilitarianism**, has become influential. The basis for this version is the need to consider what the individual would choose in a particular situation. The aim then is to seek to satisfy to the greatest degree possible everyone's preferences within that situation. One of the advantages of this is being able to avoid forcing one person's understanding of happiness on another. (For example, the Government of a rich country could develop an aid policy for poorer countries, based on the understanding of happiness among the inhabitants of those poorer countries rather than on the economic goals of the inhabitants of the rich country. In this way it could aim to satisfy to the greatest extent the possible preferences of the majority in the situation.)

Evaluating Utilitarianism

Mel Thompson[11] suggests that Utilitarianism can be criticised for a number of reasons:

- **The concept of happiness is so wide that it can change completely from one person to another.**

    Since it has such a personal basis, it could be argued that Utilitarianism does not offer any objective guidelines for deciding whether a particular act is morally good or morally wrong. What makes me happy may make you unhappy. So how can we come to an ethical decision? Some have, therefore, argued that it does not offer an independent ethical theory, but rather is completely dependent on the personal values of the individuals within the situation.

- **The use of the happiness of the majority as an ethical principle does not provide any help in some situations.**

  For example, if the choice for hospital managers is between earmarking funds to pay for a heart transplant for one middle-aged man and paying for artificial knees for ten retired patients, what help does Utilitarianism offer? What decision would, in this case, offer 'the greatest happiness to the greatest number'?

- **Utilitarianism is dependent on our ability to know what gives the greatest happiness to the greatest number or what will be for their general good.**

  What makes me happy today may make me unhappy in ten years time. And, in any case, how can I know, without asking them, what will give the greatest number the greatest happiness?

- **Utilitarianism cannot account for those situations where a person feels that a particular act is morally right whatever its consequences.**

  Utilitarianism would tend to conclude that a person - for example, a doctor - should seek to save a person's life only on condition that

  (a)   there was a fair degree of certainty that the person's life would in fact be saved and that

  (b)   the saving of that person's life would in fact ensure 'the greatest happiness for the greatest number'.

But is it not my responsibility to try to save a person's life whatever the consequences of that attempt? This means that Utilitarianism does not recognise the moral value of the act itself, but only of its consequences in terms of the greatest happiness of the majority.

- **G. E. Moore (in his Principia Ethica, 1903) criticises Mill for equating 'good' and 'desirable'.**

In chapter 3 he writes:

> 'The fact is that "desirable" does not mean "able to be desired" as "visible" means "able to be seen". The desirable means simply what ought to be desired or deserves to be desired or what is good to desire...'[12]

In other words, Mill refers to 'ought' when he should refer to what is desirable. The fact that it is possible to desire something does not mean that it should be desired.

- *By aiming to offer objective ethical guidelines a person is asked to set aside any personal values and beliefs.*
  Bernard Williams (*in Utilitarianism: For and Against, CUP, 1973*) argues that the basis for morality is a set of personal values and projects, which become the basis for deciding how a person acts. It is morally unacceptable that Utilitarianism expects a person to set aside personal commitments and values in order to serve the greatest happiness of the majority. According to this view, a moral theory that undermines personal integrity is morally unacceptable.

- *The problem of special responsibilities challenges Utilitarianism.* Most people would admit that we have certain responsibilities towards other people, whether or not they contribute to the sum of human happiness. For example, two people are drowning and you can save only one of them. One is a famous scientist whose work is developing cures for certain types of cancers. The other person is your father. Who should you try to save? The scientist would probably make a greater contribution to the sum of human happiness, and from a utilitarian point of view should be the one you try to save. On the other hand, the other person is your father; surely you have a special, personal responsibility to save him! Utilitarianism does not offer much help in making an ethical decision in this situation.

- *The problem of justice also challenges Utilitarianism.* Utilitarianism encourages us to seek the greatest happiness of the greatest number, but what if this overall growth in happiness creates considerable inequalities and injustices? Can these be justified for the sake of the majority? To take another example, what if a judge (when capital punishment was a legal sentence in law) were to sentence to death a person he knew to be innocent, because the judge believed that this would offer an example to others and lead to greater freedom and happiness for the population at large? Does the greater freedom and happiness of the majority justify the death of an innocent person? If the principle of utility does not help us in making decisions about justice, then we need to use other principles which do not only employ the measure of consequences and effects.

Chapter 3

Tasks

Writing tasks	1. (a) Is happiness an adequate basis for an ethical theory?
	(b) Does distinguishing between 'superior happiness' and 'inferior happiness' help to define happiness?
	2. You are responsible for the funds of a large hospital. You have a choice between spending £75,000 either on one surgical treatment (to perform a heart-transplant on one middle-aged man who is the father of three young children and who has been a heavy smoker throughout his adult life) or spending the same sum on a hip-replacement operation for ten people over 70 years old. You have decided to use the principles of Utilitarianism to make your decision.
	(a) Outline the main principles of Utilitarianism.
	(b) Which aspects of Utilitarianism are most helpful in this situation?
	3. 'An act has no moral value in itself. Its moral worth can only be measured in terms of the consequences of the act.'
	Evaluate this view.

Glossary

ambiguity	having a double meaning: it could mean this or it could mean that
predictive	a way of thinking or reasoning which seeks to calculate in advance what the results of a particular act would be
spiritual	relating to an understanding of, and responses to, beings and realities that are beyond physical existence

Situation Ethics

Aim

After studying this chapter, you should be able to understand and interpret Situation Ethics, its characteristics and principles. You should also be able to assess whether this ethical approach has relevance today.

It will enable you to compare and contrast Situation Ethics, Natural Law and Utilitarianism, being aware of the principle of proportionalism, which can be seen as bringing together aspects of Natural Law and Situation Ethics. Finally you will be encouraged to apply Situation Ethics to contemporary situations and issues.

The beginnings: Joseph Fletcher

Situation Ethics was developed by **Joseph Fletcher (1905 – 1991)**, an Anglican priest in the USA, who published his book of the same title in 1966. The essential point of this ethic is:

- **to reject absolute moral rules or laws which should be applied in all situations;**

- **to insist that there is only one principle for Christian morality, namely, the law of love, and this is the only absolute rule;**

- **therefore, in any particular situation, the right thing to do is what love demands.**

In the words of **Archbishop William Temple (1881-1944)**:

> 'There is only one ultimate and invariable duty, and its formula is 'Thou shalt love thy neighbour as thyself'. How to do this is another question, but this is the whole of moral duty.'[13]

The meaning of love

Love is extremely difficult to define since the word is used in so many ways. It can refer to emotion or feeling; it can mean loving action; it could be understood as a combination of reason, emotion and action.

> **Seminar topic**
>
> *Is an absolute moral law essential to a healthy society?*

What is love?

The basis for Fletcher's definition of the fundamental principle of love is the Greek term 'agape'. This is used almost without exception in the New Testament to refer to God's love for us and the love we should have for God and our neighbour.

One of the best descriptions of this love is that of St. Paul:

> 'Love is patient; love is kind; love is not envious or boastful or arrogant or rude. It does not insist on its own way; it is not irritable or resentful; it does not rejoice in wrongdoing, but rejoices in the truth. It bears all things, believes all things, hopes all things, endures all things.'
>
> (I Corinthians 13: 4-7)

So Thompson comments:

> '...it is not a self-indulgent emotion that happens to have latched onto an external object, but a recognition of that object as separate from oneself but held to be of value.'[14]

Thus Fletcher's basic principle is: 'there is nothing which is good in itself except love.'

He quotes St. Augustine: to know whether a person is good or not 'we do not ask in what he believes or in what he hopes but rather what does he love?'

Seminar topic

Discuss this quotation from St. Augustine. Do you agree?

The characteristics of love

Fletcher outlines the characteristics of love in terms of six fundamental principles. If the demands of love in every situation are to be followed, the following principles must be applied:

- **Only one thing is intrinsically good: that is, love and nothing else**

- **The ruling norm of Christian decision-making is love and nothing else**

- **Love and justice are the same. Justice is love distributed**

- **Love wills the neighbour's good whether we like him/her or not**

- **Only the end justifies the means**

- **Love's decisions are made situationally and not prescriptively.**

Task

Writing task	Apply these fundamental principles to sex before marriage. What conclusions would you draw?

The working principles of Situation Ethics

Vardy and Grosch[15] summarise the four working principles of Situation Ethics as follows:

PRAGMATISM: The act must be pragmatic i.e. practicable.

It is essential that the act under consideration has practical consequences. That is, it must be likely that the act will achieve its aims. How can it be decided whether or not it is likely to work? Only by setting a goal or target for the act. According to Fletcher, the basis for judging the success or failure of any thought or act is: Does it serve the purposes of love?

RELATIVISM: It is essential to act on the basis of relativism rather than absolutism.

Situation Ethics rejects phrases such as 'never' or 'always' since different circumstances always create exceptions. But this does not mean that people can do whatever they like, because they must always act in a way which is consistent with the law of love. Deciding how to act lovingly will depend on the situation.

POSITIVISM: It is essential to make a deliberate decision in favour of the claim of faith that 'God is love'.

That is, an individual must decide in favour of Christian love, love which cannot be verified by reason:

'Situation Ethics depends on a free decision by individuals to give first place to Christian love - this, therefore, rests on a fundamental value judgement which cannot be rationally proven.'[16]

PERSONALISM: It is essential to give priority to persons.

People must come first. While the primary question for Natural Law is: What does the law say? Situation Ethics asks: What is of greatest assistance to people?

Seminar topic

You are members of a government appointed Commission entrusted with the task of reducing the number of divorces in Britain. Apply the above working principles, namely, pragmatism, relativism, positivism and personalism, to develop responses to the following questions:

(a) Is it practicable to seek to reduce divorces?

(b)   Would such a programme of divorce reduction be consistent with 'the law of love'?

(c)   Which would be of greatest assistance to people generally in Britain, reducing the number of divorces or making divorce easier?

Having considered these responses, consider whether, as a Commission, you would still wish to bring recommendations to the government on reducing the number of divorces.

Evaluating Situation Ethics

Advantages: Thompson[17] summarises the advantages of Situation Ethics as follows:

- **It is easy to understand:** only one principle has to be applied.

- **It is flexible:** it gives one freedom to act differently from another without feeling that the act was out of place or inappropriate.

- **It enables an emotional and rational response to any situation:** there is no necessity to act according to a particular rule if a person feels deeply that to act in such a way would be contrary to the requirements of love.

- **It is based on love** which is a key characteristic of every moral system.

Disadvantages: Thompson also notes a number of disadvantages:

- **The absolute law of love is still a law.** Anyone who is going to act selfishly is just as likely to break the law of love as to break any other moral principles or rules.

- **There is a danger that it will lead to moral ambiguity** because there is no objective way of ensuring that two people will come to the same conclusion about the demands of the law of love in any particular situation.

- **It tends to sub-divide complex moral situations into individual moral decisions where the law of love must be applied.** There may come a time when it is necessary to step back, to look at the whole situation and ask, What would be all the consequences of acting in a particular way?

Other disadvantages could be added:

- **Situation Ethics is very individualistic and subjective:** it depends very much on my own response and interpretation of the rule of love and the demands of a particular situation. After all, it is often difficult to discern what the law of love demands.

- **In rejecting absolute moral laws, it could be in danger of justifying and condoning some acts, such as murder, adultery, lying and murder, that are clearly contrary to what is good.** Are these not acts which are immoral whether or not they are motivated by love? Indeed, could it not be argued that acts such as adultery or murder are contrary to the rule of law, whatever the circumstances? Or could it be argued that love could, from time to time, justify adultery or murder?

Tasks

Seminar topic

Evaluate the advantages and disadvantages of Situation Ethics compared with:

(i) Natural Law
(ii) Utilitarianism.

Presentation task	Using the results of the above discussion, use computer graphics (i) to prepare a presentation on the main features of Natural Law, Utilitarianism and Situation Ethics; (ii) to set out the advantages and disadvantages of each theory.
Writing tasks	Situation Ethics claims that 'acting according to the absolute law of love' is an adequate basis for developing a moral theory. (a) Outline briefly the six characteristics or fundamental principles of Situation Ethics. (b) Explain 'the absolute law of love'. How may its demands vary from situation to situation? Give examples to illustrate your answer.
	An unmarried and unemployed mother of three young children is offered a substantial sum of money by a wealthy married man, on condition that she has sexual intercourse with him. (a) Outline briefly what moral guidance Natural Law or Utilitarianism or Situation Ethics would offer her. (b) What advice would you offer her and why?

Glossary

Anglican	a family of Churches which have their origins in the Church of England, which was established in England and Wales as a result of the sixteenth century Reformation
individualistic	concerned only about the individual and not the wider community or society
literal/over-literal	sticking to the original words or texts and their meaning / placing too much emphasis on the original texts and their meanings
prescriptively	determining or deciding in advance what would be right or appropriate
situationally	being aware of a particular situation or circumstance
St. Paul	one of the earliest apostles, missionary, founder of many of the earliest churches described in the Christian New Testament and author of letters or epistles to many of them

Ethical Precepts of the World Religions

Aim

This chapter provides basic information about the main ethical precepts (principles) of the six major world religions. At AS level you are required to study one major world religion. After studying the appropriate section of the chapter about your chosen religion, you should

- *have an understanding of the way in which ethics are rooted in religious texts, religious traditions, and religious authorities;*

- *be able to determine how religious concepts affect moral attitudes and principles;*

- *be aware of the relationship between absolutist rules and principles and personal feelings and circumstances;*

- *have a recognition of the role of conscience and reason in relation to ethical precepts; and*

- *have an understanding of the diversity of ethical attitude and behaviour.*

Introduction: Religion and Morality

This chapter will explore in some detail the relationship between religion and morality. It will focus on each of the six major world religions in turn. Before proceeding, it is suggested that students remind themselves of some of the issues raised towards the end of chapter 1. In particular, it would be helpful to read the responses to the following questions:

- On what basis do individuals and society make ethical decisions?

- Are absolute positions on moral matters possible or acceptable in a post-religious society?

- What is the relationship between religion and ethics?

Class discussion

Three possibilities are suggested in response to this last question, namely,

- Morality depends on religion
- Morality and religions are interdependent
- Morality and religion are independent

Examine these options and seek to decide which view is most valid.

5.1   Buddhism[18]

Buddhism is rooted in the example and teaching of the Buddha (Siddhartha), a prince who lived in North India during the sixth century BCE. Caught up in the philosophical and religious issues of his time, he became very disturbed by some of the beliefs, rituals and practices. He was particularly concerned about questions of suffering and the eternal questions of life and death.

So he set about exploring some of these philosophical issues and experimenting with different lifestyles and techniques of meditation. At the age of 35, during a period of meditation, after almost despairing of finding any answers, he attained enlightenment and saw into the nature of things. He realised that everything is impermanent, including the self, and that ignorance of this results only in suffering.

Following his enlightenment he devoted himself to teaching and preaching to others - to all classes of people within Indian society. The foundation of Buddhist ethics lies in the Buddha's teaching on ethical issues.

5.1.1. Religious texts, traditions and authorities

Texts

First and foremost, then, Buddhism is founded on the discourses of the Buddha. But it also includes ethical reflections found in later Buddhist traditions. Initially, these discourses were handed down through an oral tradition and it was not until the first century BCE that the monks wrote them down on leaves.

These discourses from the Pali Canon can be subdivided into three 'baskets':

•   rules of discipline for monks (Vinaya Pitaka);

•   the basic teachings of the Buddha (Sutta Pitaka);

•   a later system of doctrine developed by later commentators (Abidhamma Pitaka).

These texts contain what is known as dharma (Buddhist teaching) and, therefore, are the authoritative texts and primary sources of Buddhism. In addition to the Pali Canon, there is a huge body of Sanskrit literature, attributed to the Buddha. What the historical Buddha may or may not have said is not clear. In Buddhism, however, if a teaching is attributed to him and it helps people in the quest for enlightenment, then it has authority.

Traditions

The earliest tradition[19] of Buddhism is known as Theravada Buddhism (the way of the elders) and became established especially in South East Asia. This tradition focuses on:

- the figure of the Buddha, not as a god to be worshipped but as one who shares our humanity;
- the celebration of his unique and great achievement in teaching the way of enlightenment;
- the Buddha as a model and inspiration for ordinary human beings.

In this tradition, then, there is a uniqueness about the spiritual and ethical example and teaching of the Buddha that is a model for those who follow his path.

A later tradition, Mahayana Buddhism (the greater Vehicle) is more concerned than Theravada Buddhism with the notion of achieving enlightenment, and was developed by later followers of the Buddha. This tradition focuses on:

- the Buddha as one among many enlightened beings;
- the potential of all human beings to become enlightened Buddhas;
- the key notion of connectedness, between ourselves and others and between ourselves and the natural world, as the ultimate truth;
- nirvana not as a far-off goal but as implicit in the here and now;
- the bodhisattva path through stages toward wisdom and enlightenment.

In the Mahayana tradition, the teachings of the Buddha and his successors are offered to enable all human beings to achieve spiritual and ethical enlightenment by following the bodhisattva path.

Authority

The teachings of the Buddha and the teachers who developed the philosophical underpinning of Buddhism (dharma) are authoritative in the sense that they are the foundation of Buddhism and are the source of Buddhist belief and practice. However, the Buddha did not require that those who would follow this path towards enlightenment should obey everything that he and his successors taught. These teachings are offered as guidance for spiritual and moral development and enlightenment. Different people at different levels of spiritual attainment, at different times and in different contexts, will respond in different ways and to different degrees to these teachings and will reach different levels of attainment.

How important are statues of the Buddha in providing a focus for reflection on behaviour for Buddhists?

5.1.2. Religious concepts and moral attitudes

Buddhist dharma includes a number of key concepts:

(a) **Karma:** The understanding of karma ('the correlation between intentions, actions and their consequences in the life or future lives of the individual.'[20]) is the key to Buddhist dharma. The Buddha contributed an ethical and psychological orientation to karma which emphasised not people's actions in themselves but rather the intentions and motivations behind actions. So the key question is not primarily, 'What should I do?' or 'What did she do?' but 'What are my intentions?' or 'Why did she do it?'. This is not to say that the acts or deeds themselves are not ethically important, but rather to emphasise that the intentions or motives behind an act or deed are just as ethically significant as the act or deed itself.

(b) **Laksanas** (the three marks of existence): The Buddha set out the three marks of what he saw as the human condition. It is characterised by:

- *dukkha*: often translated as suffering but probably best defined as 'the absence of total, perfect, unalloyed happiness'.[21] According to Wendy Dossett:

> 'Dukkha is a description of the human condition. It touches everything, even happiness. The Buddha never denied that it was possible to be happy in life (in fact, he himself had been very happy while in his father's palace), he just denied that this happiness was eternal. Because no happiness is ever permanent, all happiness is 'tainted'... This 'taint' is dukkha.'

- *anicca/anitya*: impermanence i.e. no person and no object remains forever, everything is constantly changing, everything is in flux.

- *anatta/anatman*: even the self, or soul, or essence of a person is changing, and is impermanent.

The moral attitudes and ethical teaching of Buddhism are shaped by these three characteristics of human life.

Class discussion

How do these three concepts of 'suffering', the impermanence of all things, and the impermanence of the self, influence ethical decisions?

(c) **The Five Precepts:** Buddhism offers five precepts or training rules/goals to enable those who follow the path to develop spiritually and morally:

- I undertake to abstain from harming
- I undertake to abstain from taking anything which is not given
- I undertake to abstain from misuse of the senses
- I undertake to abstain from misuse of speech
- I undertake to abstain from taking any substance which clouds the mind.

(d) **The Four Noble Truths:** These are offered to enable Buddhists to find the path towards enlightenment and liberation from the human condition as defined by 'the three marks of existence'. They have been described as 'a doctor's diagnosis of the human condition and a prescription for its cure'.[22] The Four Noble Truths are:

- The existence of dukkha (suffering) must be acknowledged;
- Suffering is caused by craving, greed and desire;
- Suffering can be brought to an end;
- The way to end suffering is to follow the Eightfold Path.

(e) **The Eightfold Path:** This sets out a set of inter-related spiritual and ethical principles by which a Buddhist may progress and develop. They are not commandments to be obeyed. They are offered as a way out of the human condition. The path can be set out in three sections as follows:

Wisdom
Right understanding (of the Buddha's teaching of impermanence and no permanent self)

Right thought (intentions and motives are as important as acts)

Morality
Right speech (a careless word can cause harm or damage)

Right action (actions always have consequences, and behind actions are motives)

Right livelihood (an occupation should be founded on ethical principles and should not harm others)

Meditation
Right effort (the path to enlightenment is difficult and so considerable effort is needed to attain it)

Right mindfulness (being aware of one's inner motivations and the consequences of one's actions)

Right concentration (by using meditation to gain insight into truth and the path to enlightenment).

Seminar topic

'Buddhism is a vast and diverse religion and Buddhists interpret these precepts in a variety of different ways.' (Dossett)

Consider each of the Five Precepts in turn and for each one, suggest an example of a way in which they could be applied to an area of sexual ethics (e.g. sex before marriage, homosexuality, adultery, divorce).

How does picturing the eightfold path as an eight-spoked wheel help you to understand the relationship between the eight principles?

(f) **Connectedness:** In Mahayama Buddhism the truth of connectedness is fundamental. Human beings belong together across time and space. Human beings are also part of the created universe or the natural world. All is connected. This calls for wisdom and compassion to see that all ethical decisions must recognise that all is connected. Decisions I make about my immediate family must recognise our connectedness with the suffering of those who are far away. Compassion must be all-embracing.

Seminar topic

Compare the Eightfold Path with the Ten Commandments in the Hebrew Bible. In what ways are they similar; in what ways are they different?

5.1.3. Absolute rules, general principles and personal circumstances

The Buddhist dharma or teaching was not given to the Buddha's followers as a set of commandments to be obeyed, but as guidance to be followed on the path towards moral and spiritual development and enlightenment. If they proved helpful they should be followed, but if they proved to be unhelpful Buddhists should not be bound by them. In this sense, there are no absolute rules in Buddhism but rather general principles. A basic pragmatism underlies all Buddhist teaching.

The personal response to the guidance offered within the teaching is, therefore, central. Buddhists are called to act with full responsibility for the consequences of their actions.

> 'In the end, individuals are responsible for their actions and have an obligation to test the tradition by their own experience.'[23]

5.1.4. Reason and conscience:

It is clear, therefore, that reason and personal conscience play a vital role in Buddhist ethics. Since inner motives and intentions are fundamental, reason has to be used to discern these inner motives and reflect upon the theoretical and traditional Buddhist teaching from the perspective of one's own experience and discernment. Ethical action calls for reason and personal wisdom.

In the same way, conscience plays a central role. It is through applying conscience to teaching and experience that the Eightfold Path, for example, can become a guide for a moral life.

5.1.5. Diversity:

There is considerable diversity within Buddhism. First, there is a diversity of traditions. For example,

- Theravada Buddhism sees the Buddha as a unique model for human behaviour.

- Mahayana Buddhism believes that enlightenment is open to all, that all have the potential to be Buddhas and that there is a vital connectedness between all things.

Secondly, because each person is free to test the teaching in the light of conscience and personal experience, the way in which individual Buddhists live out the moral precepts of Buddhist teaching will vary from person to person, from age to age and from situation to situation.

Class discussion

Invite someone from a local Buddhist group or community to visit the class:

(a) discuss with them how they respond to Buddhist teaching in their own life;

(b) explore with them how different situations could cause them to come to different views on moral issues, for example, in relation to sexual ethics;

(c) prepare a brief report of your discussions for the school newsletter.

5.2 Christianity

Christianity is rooted within the story and faith of the Hebrew people as recorded in the Hebrew Scriptures; in the life, teaching and work of Jesus, as told in the Gospels; and as interpreted in other New Testament writings and in the tradition of the Church throughout the centuries.

Therefore, Christian ethics reflect the ethical perspectives of Judaism (for example, in the Ten Commandments) but as re-formed and re-interpreted by Jesus Christ.

5.2.1 Religious texts, traditions and authorities

Texts

All Christians regard the Bible as the Word of God, although there is considerable diversity in what they mean by this phrase. But at least it means that the Bible (which includes the Hebrew Scriptures or Old Testament and the New Testament) is the primary textual source for Christian ethics. Notably, Christians lay particular emphasis on key texts within the Old and New Testaments. For example,

- The Ten Commandments (see Exodus 20: 1-17 and Deuteronomy 5: 1-21): regarded as a basic summary of Christian morality as well as Jewish morality e.g. 'Do not murder', 'Do not commit adultery', and 'Do not steal'.

- The Sermon on the Mount (see Matthew 5 - 7): a summary of the ethical teaching of Jesus, in which Jesus re-interpreted the Ten Commandments, deepening them and making them even more demanding.

- Jesus claimed that he came to fulfil the Law (of the Old Testament) rather than to set it aside as some of his contemporaries accused him of doing (see Matthew 5: 17-20).

However, there are those who would encourage Christians to rethink their understanding of the authority of the Bible for today. For example, Bishop Richard Holloway criticises the traditional dogmatic approach to scripture that views it as free from any errors. Scripture, for example, condones slavery in a way which Christians today would completely condemn:

Class discussion

Should the Ten Commandments be restored as the moral foundation and authority of British society?

'...We should not shirk from the task of rethinking the authority of the Bible over our lives, allowing the living scripture of our own experience to challenge the dead letter of the written law... We have done this over its attitude to slavery...(but) we seem unable to make this liberating change in our attitude (for example) to human sexuality...'[24]

Tasks

Writing tasks

'Do not commit murder. Do not commit adultery. Do not steal. Do not give false evidence against your neighbour.' (Exodus 20: 13-16)

'You have heard that our forefathers were told, "Do not commit murder..."...But what I tell you is this: Anyone who nurses anger against his brother must be brought to justice.' (Matthew 5: 21-22)

(a) Explain briefly the way in which Jesus interprets the Ten Commandments in the above extract from the Sermon on the Mount.

(b) Determine whether Jesus' ethical teaching in the Sermon on the Mount is still valid today.

Traditions

There are three major traditions within Christianity, which have much in common with each other but which also display some fundamental differences. For example, each of the traditions sees the Bible as a fundamental authority for faith and behaviour, but would have different approaches to its interpretation:

- **The Catholic Church**
  - goes back to the early Western tradition of Christianity, centred in Rome;
  - the Pope, as the Bishop of Rome, is the earthly head;
  - moral teaching based on Scripture as interpreted through the teaching of the Church;
  - firmly rooted in the moral theology of St. Thomas Aquinas (1225-1274) and especially on Natural Law Theory (chapter 2).

- **The Orthodox Tradition**
  - goes back to the early Eastern tradition of Christianity;
  - Catholic and Orthodox traditions of the Christian Church were divided following the Great Schism of 1054CE;
  - the Orthodox Tradition has its centre in Constantinople (the present-day Istanbul);
  - there are many 'local' Orthodox Churches that are autonomous but which are also in full relationship with each other;
  - lays considerable emphasis on Scripture in relation to faith and morality;
  - places particular emphasis on the teaching of the seven Ecumenical Councils held during the first eight centuries CE.

- **Churches of the Reformation**
  - initiated by Luther, Calvin and Zwingli in the sixteenth century CE;
  - consists of a very large and diverse family of churches and denominations;
  - have common origins in the Reformation;
  - regard the Bible as the ultimate authority in faith and behaviour;
  - some regard the Bible as the only authority, morality being firmly rooted in biblical teaching and especially the teaching of Jesus;
  - others (e.g. the Anglican Churches) regard the Bible, the teaching of the Church and the application of reason, as forming together the source and foundation of Christian morality; the teaching of Jesus remains central but the role of the church in interpreting Scripture is also important. In this sense, these churches have much in common with the Catholic tradition.

Authority

This summary of the main Christian traditions makes it clear that there are many sources of authority for Christian morality and that they vary from church to church and from denomination to denomination. These sources of authority include:

- The authority of the Bible as the Word of God;
- The authority of the Church - understood in different ways by the different traditions - in interpreting Scripture;
- The direct inspiration of the Holy Spirit, the third 'person' of the Trinity;
- Human reason that enables human beings to understand and interpret the will of God.

Seminar topic

Contact local representatives of the three main Christian traditions within your community and invite them to describe their understanding of the sources of Christian ethics.

5.2.2. Religious concepts and moral attitudes

a) **Belief in God, Father, Son and Holy Spirit:** This primary and central Christian belief in the Trinity or the Triune God or the Three-in-One, could be expressed as 'Faith in God, Creator, Redeemer and Sanctifier'. This phrase underlines a concept that is fundamentally important in relation to Christian ethics:

- At the heart of the Christian faith is a belief in God who created the universe, giving it design and purpose: God's will is at work in the universe and can be discerned by human beings. This central belief is the basis for Aquinas' Natural Law Theory;

- Jesus was the Son of God and in his life and teaching he offers an example which his followers are called to imitate;

- The imitation of Christ is an important but impossible goal of Christian morality;

- Through the suffering, death and resurrection of Jesus Christ, God released (i.e. redeemed) human beings from all that held them captive and enabled them to become children of God. Jesus' teaching, life, suffering, death and resurrection are, therefore, central to Christian ethics;

- Christians confess Jesus Christ as Lord. One implication of this title is that Jesus is believed to be Lord over all things;

- Thus Christians have a responsibility to work out in their individual lives as well as in society as a whole the lordship of Christ over the whole of life;

- God the Holy Spirit is at work in the world and within human beings enabling them to discern the will of God as revealed in Jesus Christ, and transforming (or sanctifying) human beings in 'the image of God' (see Genesis 1: 26).

Is a Christian belief in God as Father, Son and Holy Spirit essential to Christian ethics?

b) **Sin:** Christians believe that human beings are fundamentally sinful. This phrase is understood in a number of ways within the Christian tradition:

- Commonly used to mean 'doing wrong' e.g. stealing, killing, or breaking the commandments;

- Disobedience to God's law as set out in the Bible or more generally disobedience to the revealed will and purpose of God;

- 'Falling short of the glory of God' (St. Paul in Romans 3: 23), that is, failing to live up to what God intended us to be as beings created 'in the image of God';

- Theologically, the condition that causes human beings to be 'alienated from God' or 'separated from God' and subject to the power of evil or the Evil One (i.e. Satan);

- 'Original sin' is traditionally used to mean that human beings are flawed from the beginning because of disobedience and 'no generation escapes its effects';[25]

- May be understood not only in terms of individual failure and alienation but also in terms of collective sinfulness e.g. the sin of a society or a nation or the sin of humankind.

Christian morality takes sin seriously as an explanation for the human condition. The Christian faith affirms that through Christ God offers a way of escaping the effects of sin (salvation or redemption) and a moral framework within which individuals and society may be transformed.

c) **Love:** At the heart of Christian ethics is the Christian understanding of love. The Greek word used in the New Testament is agape. Two quotations from the New Testament illustrate what Christians mean by love:

- Jesus was once asked by a Pharisee which was the greatest commandment in the law. His answer was:

> '"Love the Lord your God with all your heart, with all your soul, and with all your mind." That is the greatest, the first commandment. The second is like it: "Love your neighbour as yourself." Everything in the law and the prophets (i.e. in the teaching of the Hebrew Scriptures) hangs on these two commandments.'
>
> Matthew 22: 37-39

So the law of love is at the heart of Jesus' teaching:

> '"Is the decision in accordance with the law of love?" Amid all the rules and regulations that can be found in the Christian tradition, this one stands supreme.'[26]

- Paul, writing to the Corinthians, describes love as 'the greatest gift':

> 'Love is patient and kind. Love envies no one, is never boastful, never conceited, never rude; love is never selfish, never quick to take offence. Love keeps no secret of wrongs, takes no pleasure in the sins of others, but delights in the truth. There is nothing that love cannot face; there is no limit to its faith, its hope, its endurance.'
>
> I Corinthians 13: 4-7

- Love as understood in these key passages is at the heart of Christian ethics.

- In Situation Ethics, love became the key principle (chapter 4); 'There is only one absolute moral law, namely, the law of love.' (Fletcher).

d) **The Kingdom of God:** According to Mark's Gospel, Jesus' first sermon was, 'The time has arrived; the kingdom of God is upon you. Repent and believe the gospel.' The kingdom was central to Jesus' teaching. It had many dimensions but it had a particularly powerful ethical significance:

- Its roots went back to the Old Testament, especially to the message of the eighth century BCE prophets of Judah, like Isaiah and Amos, who called God's people to live in justice, equality and mercy.

- It also reflected the concerns of Isaiah 61 which announces that the Spirit of God is upon the unknown prophet who is sent to proclaim good news to the poor, sight to the blind, freedom to the oppressed and liberty for those in captivity.

- The song of Mary (the Magnificat, Luke 1: 46-55) picks up this theme and rejoices that the one to whom Mary will give birth 'will bring down the mighty from their thrones and lift up the humble.'

- These themes are taken up in Luke 4: 16-20 when Jesus preached in the synagogue in Nazareth, announcing that those words of Isaiah 61 had been fulfilled in him.

- Similarly, the Beatitudes in Matthew 5: 1-12, which are part of the Sermon on the Mount, promise that those who are poor in spirit, those who are merciful, those who mourn, those who are peacemakers and those who hunger and thirst for justice will receive the blessings of the kingdom of God.

These themes of social justice and social transformation are important thrusts of Jesus' ethical teaching and have become central aspects of Christian social ethics throughout the centuries. There is at the heart of Christian moral teaching a radical challenge to all people and powers that oppress, and create unjust and unequal societies. They are reminders that Christian ethics are not just about individual behaviour and lifestyle but also about social justice and social transformation.

Task

Research task	Read the following passages: Luke 4: 16-20, Matthew 5: 1-12 and Luke 6: 20-32.
	List the key aspects of a Christian ethic that can be traced to these passages.

5.2.3. Absolute rules, general principles and personal circumstances

If these are the basic religious concepts that underpin Christian ethics, does Christianity offer absolute moral values that are true for all times and places and people?

- Christian moral values do have an absolute character. For example, Christians believe - with Judaism - that the Ten Commandments have been given by God and that they require complete obedience.

- Jesus went further and called for obedience to an even harder set of ethical demands.

- But the development of Christian ethics also provides many examples of Christian theologians and moralists claiming to use human reason to argue for ethical positions that seem to contradict the demands of Jesus' teaching.

  An example of this is the attitude to war. Some Christians have taken the commandment 'You shall not kill' to be not just a prohibition on murder but also a prohibition on capital punishment, on killing another person in self-defence or on killing soldiers and civilians in war and conflict. This principle, known as pacifism, has been a long-standing ethical position within the Church. At the same time, there have been other Christian leaders and theologians who have argued equally powerfully that this commandment is not a ban on all killing but merely a prohibition of murder in cold blood. They have developed a carefully argued case for what is known as 'just war', claiming that this position is perfectly in agreement with Biblical and Christian ethics. Which position is correct? Can both be equally acceptable?

- Similarly, the commandment to love God and one another is central to Christian ethics. Jesus claims that these sum up the whole of the Law. Does this take the place of the demands of the Law? If we love in this way, can Christians forget about the commandments? What should be the relationship between moral rules and the law of love? Situation Ethics is one response to this age-old dilemma.

- What do Christians do when their own perception of Christian truth and ethics tells them that one action is right and the authority of the Church demands that they do something entirely opposite?

  For example, the Catholic Church has declared that any contraception by artificial means is contrary to the Law of God and the teaching of the Church. Therefore, they expect members of the Church to follow this absolute rule. Many - perhaps the majority within the Catholic Church - obey this demand. However, it is well known that many married people within the Church reject this view completely and use artificial contraception, in all conscience believing it to be consistent with Christian morality. Who is right, those who obey the Church authorities or those who follow the leading of their Christian conscience? It is clear that in Christian morality there is a constant tension between authority and personal responsibility. How can this be resolved?

5.2.4. Reason and conscience

'Conscience stands for each individual as absolutely and solely responsible before God for the formation of her or his decision, thought or action...No authority...can invade that conscience to control or coerce it. Each person stands before God.'[27]

Class discussion

Do Christian ethics make absolute demands?

Dietrich Bonhoeffer, a German theologian who was executed in April 1945 for his involvement in a failed plot to assassinate Hitler, argued that for a Christian, obedience to Jesus Christ is paramount. He writes: 'Jesus Christ has become my conscience.'

Reason also plays a central role in Christian ethics. We have already seen that reason is a key element of Natural Law Theory. The will and purpose of God can be discerned through human reason as well as from revelation. The Catholic tradition, in particular, has laid particular emphasis on the place of reason in 're-examining the relevance of particular teachings to changing cultural and social circumstances.'[28] Other traditions have rejected the place of reason and have emphasised instead the direct inspiration of the Holy Spirit.

Task

Writing task	'Ethics are all about conscience and not about rules and laws.' Evaluate this view.

5.2.5 Diversity

It is clear from this review of Christian ethical precepts that there is considerable diversity within the Christian family on moral principles and action:

- Some would see the Ten Commandments and the moral teaching of Jesus as definitive and authoritative for all Christians at all times and in all situations.

- Others would regard the ethical teaching of the Bible as setting out general principles and approaches for moral behaviour, and that the injunction of Jesus to live on the basis of love, mercy, compassion, justice and equality needs to be worked out according to one's situation and personal circumstances.

- Some would lay greatest emphasis on the Christian tradition, rooted in the Bible and handed down through the centuries, and on the way in which the social teaching of the Church, through its authoritative leadership, has interpreted that tradition for each generation.

- Others would place greater emphasis on the Bible itself as the authoritative word of God and the final judge on matters of faith and morality.

This diversity of approaches leads inevitably to a range of views on ethical issues. For example, some would make an absolute claim, on the basis of Christian tradition, that homosexual practice should always be regarded as immoral in all circumstances. Others would claim, rather like the approach of Situation Ethics, that there should be a much more open and accepting attitude to homosexual practice, and that the key question here is: What is the demand of the law of love in this situation?

Class discussion

> Invite leaders of local Christian churches to visit the class:
>
> (a) discuss with them how they respond to Christian teaching in their own lives;
>
> (b) explore with them how different situations could cause them to come to different views on moral issues, for example, in relation to sexual ethics;
>
> (c) prepare a brief report of your discussions for the school newsletter.

5.3 Hinduism

5.3.1 Texts, traditions and authorities

Hinduism is a diverse tradition in which there is a wide range of beliefs and ethical approaches. It depends as much on oral tradition as on literary sources. This section can provide only a brief summary of the key aspects of Hinduism and its approaches to ethics.

Texts

Ancient texts that are key sources for Hindu ethics and spirituality include:[29]

- **The Vedas** (c.1200BCE), a canonical collection of texts, is regarded as 'revelation' (sruti) and is the ultimate authority for Brahmanical Hinduism.[30] The principles that are 'seen' or 'heard' in these texts 'are embodied in the gods, who are models for human conduct.' The Vedic hymns tend to praise certain virtues and moral ideals such as truthfulness, giving, restraint, affection, avoiding injury to all creatures.

- **The Upanishads** develop the principles of the Vedas with a view to a more universal application.[31] They encourage a 'detached and asocial pursuit of spiritual ends removed from the challenges of the world' so that emotions are overcome in pursuit of a 'higher but nevertheless self-centred calling.' There have been charges that the tradition represents 'an ethically bankrupt …morality.' The Upanishads highlight three important virtues, namely, damyata (self-restraint), datta (giving or self-sacrifice) and dayadhvam (compassion).

- **The Dharmashastras**, which includes Manu's Law Books and Kautilya's treatise on politics. Kautilya highlights the importance of reasoning in reflection on issues of public morality. Manu notes that there are different dharma (duty) in different periods and therefore points to the possibility of ethical relativism. Manu also commends a series of virtues similar to those advocated by the Vedas (see above).

- **The Ramayana and Mahabharata**, are popular epics that explore the struggles of coming to grips with the evolving idea of dharma.

- **The Bhagavad Gita** (part of the Mahabharata), which is more decisive in its ethical pronouncements, has had an enormous influence on Hinduism. It pursues a middle course between Nivritti (abstinence: path of anti-action) and Pravatti (performative: doing of social and moral duties).

The Gita offers a model of an ethical person, in Krishna's words, as one who is:

'…without hatred of any creature, friendly and compassionate without possessiveness and self-pride, equable in happiness and unhappiness…who is dependent on nothing, disinterested, unworried… and who neither hates nor rejoices, does not mourn or hanker, and relinquishes both good and evil.'

Gita 12.13-17[32]

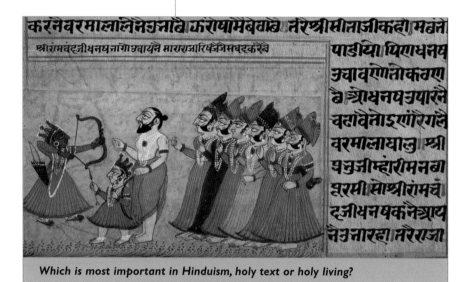

Which is most important in Hinduism, holy text or holy living?

Menski quotes Manusmiriti, the most important of the dharmashastra: 'The entire Veda is the source/root of dharma, next the smiriti literature, and the practice of people who know it, then the customs of good people, and finally one's own conscience.'[33]

He concludes, therefore, that whereas written sources may provide guidelines for ethical behaviour the individual's conscience must have the last word.

Task

Research task	Search the Internet for examples of text from the Hindu texts. Summarise one or two examples of ethical teaching that you find.

Traditions

Since the term Hinduism covers a range of diverse Indian religious traditions, it includes a wide range of views about the divine (other-worldly), the relationship between the divine and the material world and between God/god and the human soul. Hinduism believes that the one God is revealed in the form of many gods. It is also sectarian (relating to a particular group or sect). Most Hindus would probably argue that dharma is the basis of Hindu unity, since it is a sacred and eternal code which governs all aspects of life.[34] In this sense, Hinduism is defined more by action than dogma and as a result there is enormous diversity in its ethical viewpoints.[35]

Three traditions of devotion are most widely practised among Hindus:

- Shaivism, regarded by some as the oldest continuing Indian religion;[36]

- Vaishnavism, with the most followers, though divided into many subdivisions;

- Shaktism, focussed on Sakti, the Goddess and divine mother in whom all the functions … (of) Visnu … and Siva are gathered.[37]

Authority

Given the enormous diversity in Indian religious traditions and the ambiguous approach to written sources, it is not easy to identify the sources of ethical authority within Hinduism as a whole. Supreme authority rests in an invisible creative force, sometimes called God or Brahma.[38] Perhaps all that can be said is that although many scriptures can be a source of guidance on dharma and ethical behaviour, the ultimate guide for each individual believer is her or his conscience.

How does worship influence ethics?

5.3.2 Religious concepts and moral attitudes

Generally, orthopraxy (right action) is more important in Hinduism than orthodoxy (right belief). Nevertheless, there are four concepts which are fundamental to Hindu ethical behaviour:

Dharma: can be found translated as 'law', 'duty', 'righteousness' etc. It is characterised in a number of ways:

- it is understood as an eternal cosmic principle 'which controls or constrains phenomena in the universe'[39] but which is also 'responsive to different situations and contexts';

- it is central to the unity of Hinduism and incorporates the duties and ethical codes which govern all aspects of life, sacred and eternal;

- it 'emphasises the… duty of every individual to act (at all times) in such a way that righteousness is achieved; in other words, to act appropriately';[40]

- it offers guidelines for ritual obligation as well as ethical behaviour;

- it provides a form or structure of laws and regulations which become obligatory within particular cultures as well as an ethical framework for behaviour.'[41]

Within this broad understanding of the nature of dharma some very general ethical principles may be suggested:

- it is predominantly concerned with the attainment of purity or the ultimate good, which is the most desired state of being;

- it incorporates a belief in, and a ritual and ethical basis for, a cycle of reincarnation and salvation, or of liberation from states of being on the path towards purity;

- it emphasises the maintenance of balance or harmony as a basic aim of human life;

- consequently, while stressing the importance of individual conscience and freedom, there is also a strong emphasis on the inter-relatedness of human beings. In this sense, therefore, it has a strong social dimension.

In summary, Flood describes dharma as follows:

> 'It refers both to a cosmic, eternal principle and…operates within particular situations that require moral choice. Dharma is the context within which moral choice operates… These moral choices are constrained by a person's location in a hierarchical and gender-specific social structure.'[42]

Varna: Literally meaning 'colour', this describes the ancient division of society into four class or caste groups (which are in turn sub-divided into many smaller occupational groups or jati), which Thompson describes as follows:[43]

- **Brahmin:** the priestly class, generally the most highly educated and traditionally much involved with education and religion.

- **Kshatriya:** traditionally the warrior class, these tend to be involved in military and administrative posts and in the law.

- **Vaishya:** the 'merchant' class, often involved with business and agriculture.

- **Shudra:** the class for manual workers.

The varna system takes on not just a social and economic significance but also has a ritual meaning. In recent times, it has been undergoing gradual change, especially in public life, and has been the target of pressures for reformation, from within Hinduism itself as well as from outside. 'Below' the four classes are those who are outside the class system. Often referred to in English as 'untouchables', they prefer the term 'dalit', which means 'oppressed', and which, they argue, better reflects their status.

In terms of ethical behaviour, a person's status within this class structure determines to a considerable degree their understanding of dharma, their sense of duty and responsibility. The class system promotes different approaches to, and expectations of, ethics. Its intention is to foster diversity rather than inequality. Nevertheless, the class system is often seen as discriminatory, although discrimination on the basis of class is illegal in India itself.

Ashrama: These are the four stages in life, each with its own expectations and duties in relation to moral behaviour:[44]

(1) **Student:** at this stage a person is receiving instruction and is expected to show respect to parents and teachers and to exercise self-discipline. They should abstain from sex, alcohol, tobacco and drugs.

(2) **Householder:** at this stage the focus of a person's life must be marriage, family and career. 'Domesticity and its implied moral codes become more important than renunciation.'[45] Such a person has three goals of life or three paths: 'the fulfilling of social and moral obligations (dharma), becoming prosperous, and the experience of pleasure.'[46]

(3) **Retired:** traditionally, when the first grandchild arrives, the grandparents are expected to start withdrawing from family and business responsibilities and consider handing over control to the next generation.

(4) **Ascetic:** a few Hindus, in this final stage of their life, choose to renounce all their possessions and devote themselves to seeking spiritual liberation (moksha).

Karma: This term initially referred to religious ritual but came to mean action generally and its consequences, not only in 'this' life but over several lifetimes. It offers an explanation for human suffering and encouragement to break the cycle of reincarnation by seeking liberation.[47]

Manu indicates that these consequences can be 'auspicious or inauspicious' (favourable or unfavourable), according to the fulfilment of the dharma for a particular caste and stage of life. For example, at the heart of the karma of a 'householder' is the attempt to keep control of the actions of body, speech and mind.

Flood further suggests[48] that there are three kinds of karma:

- the effects of actions performed in a previous life which have not yet begun to be manifested;

- effects of previous actions which become manifested in one's present life;

- the seeds of actions sown in this life which will bear fruit in a future life.

5.3.3. Absolute rules, general principles and personal circumstances

The above outline of the Hindu approach to ethical teaching and behaviour makes it clear that, on the one hand, dharma offers 'a cosmic, eternal principle', a Natural Law, with its obligation to fulfil one's duty within a particular caste and stage of life. On the other hand, the expectations of dharma do vary according to caste and stage of life. So while duty and the hierarchical social structure are absolute and sacred, they must, at the same time, adapt to the everyday reality of making moral decisions. Indeed, Flood claims that correct action is more important than correct belief. The key concern is to take responsibility, for family and society, and to fulfil ritual obligations.[49]

Class discussion

How do dharma, varna, ashrama and karma influence ethical decisions?

5.3.4 Reason and conscience

The place of reason and conscience varies from tradition to tradition within Hinduism. But in general it could be said that, although scriptures or written sources are important as foundations for ethical principles and behaviour, considerable emphasis is placed on the individual conscience, as a person seeks to act appropriately within his or her caste or stage of life. Indeed, Menski claims[50] that the individual conscience is the most important influence in deciding ethical behaviour and that scripture actually plays a secondary role.

This approach does have its advantages:

* flexibility within diverse situations and personal circumstances;

* gives personal freedom but not complete liberty to act;

* any individual action takes into consideration wider implications, since the individual is always seen as a small part of a larger whole.

It is clear, therefore, that the place of reason in ethical decision-making will also vary considerably. Those who emphasise the guidance of scriptural sources will obviously use the resources of human reason to decide what actions are appropriate for their caste and stage of life. Some of the scriptures, such as the dharmashastras, lay particular emphasis on the use of reason in moral decision-making, especially in the public sphere.

5.3.5. Diversity

Everything that has been said in this section so far points to the enormous diversity that is at the heart of Hinduism. A number of key aspects of Hinduism point to this:

* It is a religion in which the cosmic creative force, God or Brahma, takes many forms.

* It is founded upon many scriptures.

* It has a number of traditions, including those which focus on Siva, Visnu and Sakti.

* Its moral precepts (dharma and karma) vary according to caste and stage of life.

* It places considerable emphasis on individual conscience and personal circumstances.

Class discussion

Invite someone from a local Hindu group or community to visit the class:

(a) discuss with them how they respond to Hindu teaching in their own life;

(b) explore with them how different situations could cause them to come to different views on moral issues; for example, in relation to sexual ethics;

(c) prepare a brief report of your discussions for the school newsletter.

5.4 Islam

5.4.1 Texts, traditions and authorities

Texts

The Qur'an, the sacred text of Muslims, is fundamental to Islam since it contains the complete and final revelation of the will of Allah (God), given through the prophet Muhammad. It is believed to have been revealed to Muhammad between 610 and 632 CE, recited by him and subsequently written down in Arabic.

Because the Qur'an is the revealed will of Allah, spoken by Allah, its content is generally believed to be eternal, uncreated and perfect. It is, therefore, a holy and sacred text. The Qur'an contains a range of styles of literature, including

* appeals to the hearers

* sermons

* stories and narrative accounts

* legislation.

The Qur'an is the main source of Islamic religious and ethical teaching and legislation e.g. in areas such as the central belief in the oneness of Allah, marriage and divorce, the conduct of warfare, worship and fasting. It is believed that the Qur'an reveals God's straight path and that it offers guidance in all areas of life. Therefore, there is a moral responsibility to follow this straight path, to do what is right, good and just, and to do so in all areas of life.

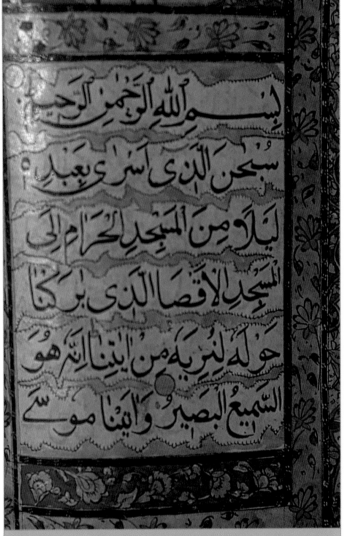

What is the significance of the Qur'an for the ethical behaviour of Muslims?

Task

Research task	Search the Internet for examples of text from the Qur'an. Summarise one or two examples of ethical teaching that you find.

Traditions

(a)   The main Islamic tradition is the Hadith. This is an account - gathered during the centuries immediately after his death - of the sayings, actions and practices of Muhammad himself during the time when he was receiving the revelations from Allah recorded in the Qur'an. Since the prophet is seen as the highest example for his followers, the Hadith records intimate details of the prophet's life and is, therefore, regarded as a key source of religious and ethical guidance for his followers.

(b) On the basis of the Qur'an and the Hadith an elaborate legal code was developed known as Shari'ah. Shari'ah law is an universal law which applies the teaching of the Qur'an and the principles of Hadith to all areas of personal, social and political life. Shari'ah law is regarded as divine law which was set out by four imam during the eighth and ninth centuries.

(c) There are four classic schools of law, all founded on the teaching of the Qur'an and the Hadith, namely,

- Hanafite
- Malikite
- Hanbalite
- Shafi'ite

These four classic schools show a diversity of approaches to religious, personal and ethical matters, but all are firmly based on the teaching of the Qur'an and the Hadith.

(d) However, since all these texts have their origins in the seventh, eighth and ninth centuries, it has been necessary for the interpretation and extension of Shari'ah to take account of contemporary situations. This extension of Shari'ah is made by

- consensus (ijma)
- mental effort (ijtihad)
- analysis (qiyas)
- public welfare (masalih)

Shari'ah is sometimes also extended by fatwa, a legal opinion given by a mufti, i.e. a person who is qualified to give such a legal opinion.

Authority

Ultimate authority in Islam is rooted in Allah. The final will of Allah has been revealed in the Qur'an. The ultimate example for human beings is found in the Hadith. Shari'ah law contains the basic legislation for all areas of life. Therefore, the Qur'an, Hadith and Shariah are authoritative for Muslims. What is right or wrong (the essence of ethics) is not a matter of personal choice or opinion. Rather 'God's straight path' is set out in these authoritative sources as eternal and unchangeable truths, which dictate the life and conduct of all Muslims.

What is the relationship between worship and behaviour for Muslims?

5.4.2 Religious concepts and moral attitudes

There are a number of religious concepts which are fundamental for Islamic ethics:

(i) **God is one:** The most fundamental principle in Islam is that Allah is one. Muhammad saw that there can be no division in God. There are many 'beautiful names' for God but only one God. If God is the supreme and perfect being there can be no division, for there can be no conflict in God. From this fundamental concept of the oneness of God, the whole of Islam is derived. If God is one there can be only one divine straight path. All aspects of creation and all aspects of human life must be ordered in obedience to this one God.

(ii) **Islam is holistic i.e. it offers guidance for the whole of life:** Therefore, ethical decision-making cannot be separated from other areas of human life, for everything that human beings do and everything they are, is based on their faith in and understanding of Allah. There can be no separation between 'sacred' and 'secular' i.e. between the religious part and the other parts of life.

The will and purpose of Allah for the whole of life is revealed in the Qur'an, which contains God's 'straight path'. When a person commits himself or herself to walk this straight path it becomes a commitment to live the whole of life ethically.

<aside>
Seminar topic

How would these two fundamental concepts of the unity of God and the wholeness of Islamic teaching influence ethical decisions?
</aside>

(iii) **Accountability to God:** Muslims believe that everyone will be accountable to God on the day of judgement. This is the real force behind the moral law of Islam.

(iv) **Balance:** Islam teaches that walking this 'straight path' means living life in a balanced way; for example, balance between justice and compassion, between wealth and poverty.

(v) **Peace:** Peace (or salam) between all creatures, all people and with God is fundamental to what it means to be a Muslim. Indeed, the word 'Islam' incorporates the Arabic word for peace ('salam').

(vi) **Five pillars of Islam:** The essence of what it is to be a Muslim is summed up in 'the five pillars of Islam': these are ash'Shahada (the witness), salat (formal prayer), zakat (tithing for the poor), hajj (pilgrimage to Mecca), and sawm (fasting during Ramadan).

Seminar topic

Compare the five pillars of Islam with some of the teachings of Jesus in The Sermon on the Mount. What do they have in common? What are the differences between them?

5.4.3 Absolute rules, general principles and personal circumstances

- The Qur'an has an absolute authority over human conduct in all areas of life.

- Shari'ah law, which is derived from the Qur'an and the Hadith, sets out the ethical implications of these Islamic texts, dividing behaviour into four categories:

   fard: obligatory duties, including the five pillars of Islam;

   halal: what is permitted, including foods and drinks as well as other kinds of behaviour;

   haram: behaviour or foods which are definitely forbidden, except under certain conditions (e.g. in a medical emergency);

   niyyah: the intent behind actions is crucial: not only must an act be good, the intent behind it must also be good.

Seminar topic

'Fard, halal, haram and niyyah are fundamental to Islamic behaviour.' Suggest one way in which each of these might influence sexual behaviour.

- Personal circumstances are only relevant to ethical decision-making in Islam to the extent that every individual has to ask him- or herself how the absolute demands of Islamic teaching can be applied in their life and conduct. The demands of Islam must take priority over everything else.

5.4.4. Reason and conscience

There is scope for reason and rational choice within Islamic ethics. Indeed, Shari'ah law is the result of applying human reason to the teaching of the Qur'an and the Hadith. Mashuk ibn Ally writes that 'tempering faith with reason' is an acceptable way of discovering what the Qur'an has to say in a changing world. Human beings are, therefore, able 'to apprehend the unknown through reflection, search and discovery.'[51]

5.4.5 Diversity

There is diversity within Islam (e.g. depending on whether the Shi'ah or the Sunni schools of law are being followed or, to some extent, on the religious, cultural and political context in which Muslims live). But such diversity permits only conduct and behaviour that is consistent with the absolute teaching of the Qur'an and Shariah law.

Class discussion

Invite someone from a local Mosque to visit the class:

(a) discuss with them how they respond to Islamic teaching in their own life;

(b) explore with them whether different situations could lead to people having different views on ethical issues, for example, in relation to sexual ethics;

(c) prepare a short report of your discussions for the school newsletter.

5.5 Judaism

Being Jewish is primarily a matter of belonging to a people, obeying the will of God in the Torah and worshipping and loving the one God. Jewish ethics have been formed over the centuries from this long and complex experience of being Jewish.

5.5.1 Religious texts, traditions and authorities

Texts

A number of key texts are the foundations of Judaism and especially of Jewish morality:

- **Torah** is the primary foundation of Judaism and the most important of its religious texts. Torah means law or teaching and consists of the first five books of the Hebrew Scriptures (sometimes called 'the Pentateuch' or five books), namely, Genesis, Exodus, Leviticus, Numbers and Deuteronomy.
  Key characteristics of Torah can be identified:

  - it represents the revealed will and purpose of God, and is regarded, therefore, as the ultimate authority for Jews and held in greatest reverence;

  - since it is directly God-given it is regarded as infallible, that is, beyond error and doubt and the only ultimate authority for faith and action;

  - it contains the moral precepts and laws by which Jews are expected to live their lives;

  - it consists of 613 laws which regulate ritual, personal and social behaviour;

  - it includes the ten commandments which are central not just for Jewish ethics but also for Christian ethics (Exodus, Chapter 20);

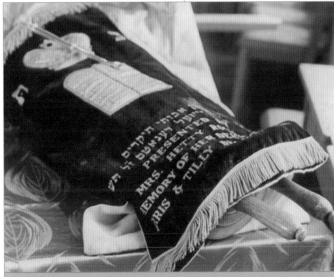

The Torah is the foundation of Judaism and is held in greatest reverence.

  - since it is an ancient text it needs interpretation and re-interpretation in order to understand its significance from generation to generation.

Seminar topic

1. **Read the Ten Commandments (Exodus 20: 1-17).**

2. **Summarise the key concerns of these Ten Commandments.**

3. **How would you defend their relevance in British society today?**

- **Books of History, Prophecy and Wisdom** are also included in the Hebrew Scriptures. These are not regarded with the same reverence as the Torah and do not have the same binding authority; nevertheless they have considerable significance in terms of the Jewish understanding of God, of their own history and of the way in which God's will is to be applied in daily life.

- **Talmud** is the second most important text in Judaism. It consists of ten encyclopaedic volumes of commentaries by rabbis and interpretations of the Torah, which were finalised in their present form around the sixth century CE. Essentially the Talmud is a record of rabbinical debates over many centuries about the way in which the law contained in the Torah should be understood and applied. Primarily, therefore, it is about how Jews should behave - the emphasis is on behaviour.

Traditions

A variety of Jewish traditions have developed over the centuries, largely based on different ways of understanding the authority of the Torah and different approaches to its interpretation. These traditions, therefore, represent different views on Jewish morality and ethics.

The traditions of Judaism include the following:

- **Orthodox:** Orthodox Jews adhere most strictly to the ancient traditions and practices of Judaism, especially with regard to the ultimate authority of the Torah. In particular, they believe that the Torah was revealed directly by God and, therefore, adhere very strictly not only to the laws of the Torah but also to the oral and written traditions (e.g. in relation to Sabbath observation and food laws).

  Orthodox Jews include a number of different groups, but one of the most prominent among them are the Hasidim, who have a distinctive dress code and are renowned for their spiritual devotion. All orthodox groups adhere to a strict code of ethical conduct based on the Torah and the Talmud.

To what extent is extreme orthodoxy an important witness to a religious faith and morality today?

- **Non-orthodox Jews**: Groups of non-orthodox Jews have developed as a response to increasing questioning of traditional approaches to the Torah. For example, they have recognised that biblical studies, especially during the twentieth century, have raised questions about the traditional belief that the whole Torah was handed down directly by God to Moses on Mount Sinai in a complete and perfect form. Questions have been raised too about some of the traditional approaches to ethics and morality. Similarly, there have been questions about whether traditional forms of worship pay enough regard to the need to be relevant to modern life and modern society.

Two streams are particularly important among non-orthodox Jews:

Conservative Judaism is largely an American phenomenon, and covers a range of beliefs and practices. Essentially it recognises that Judaism has to change in response to social and cultural change. Thus, while continuing to regard the Torah and Talmud as central and fundamental, there is also agreement to 'accept the results of modern scholarship... that historical development of the tradition has taken place and that the tradition has continued to develop. (They) agree on the indispensability of Jewish law, but a law which responds to changing times and changing needs.'[52]

Reform Judaism arose in the nineteenth century, mainly as a result of Jews living freely among Gentile (i.e. non-Jewish) communities and receiving Western education. They transformed their liturgy, used local languages as well as Hebrew, and had a more liberal approach to many of the traditional laws about food, clothing and daily living. Many of the early reformists saw themselves as 'calling the people back to a more ethical way of life...'[53]. Today Reform Jews are very much absorbed into their surrounding communities, have a slightly more traditional approach to worship than their radical founders, remain committed to equality between men and woman (and indeed have female rabbis) and put particular emphasis on ethical, rather than ritual, aspects of Judaism.

Lavinia and Dan Cohn-Sherbok illustrate the ethical differences between these traditions with reference to marriage breakdown. Traditionally, if a marriage breaks down and a civil divorce has been granted, the wife is still tied to the husband unless he agrees to grant her a religious divorce. The traditions described above would respond to contemporary examples of this situation in different ways:

- *Orthodox Judaism* would recognise the injustice of the situation but would have difficulty in doing anything.

- *Conservative Jews* have found an example in the Talmud and have written into marriage contracts a clause which declares that a marriage would be

How important is it that traditions about worship or ethics should be reformed in response to cultural and social changes?

declared null and void if, in these circumstances, a husband refuses to grant a religious divorce.

- *Reform Jews* would regard the law as out of date and unjust to women and, therefore, should be disregarded.

Tasks

| **Writing tasks** | (a) Provide a brief summary of the ethical approaches of the three streams of Jewish tradition, namely, Orthodox Judaism, Conservative Judaism and Reform Judaism. |
| | (b) Discuss which of these provides the most acceptable approach to morality today. |

Authority

The above outline of traditions within Judaism indicates that there are a number of inter-related understandings of authority within Judaism:

- The ultimate authority for faith and practice is the Torah.

- The Talmud, as the interpretation of the Torah, is a fundamental resource for deciding how Jews should obey the Torah.

- Rabbis (and scholars) within their community or together within their region have considerable authority in interpreting the Torah and the Talmud for their people.

- Different traditions will have different views on the degree to which the details of the teaching of the law in the Torah and the Talmud should have binding authority on Jews today.

- Within contemporary Judaism, therefore, there is a tension between those who believe that sacred text has final and binding authority and those who believe that sacred and authoritative text should be interpreted by the Jewish community in the light of their own situation and experience.

Class discussion

Is the only legitimate basis for morality a sacred text that has final and binding authority?

5.5.2 Religious concepts and moral attitudes

- **God is one** is the most fundamental belief of Judaism. This is repeated many times during synagogue worship: 'Hear, Israel; the Lord is our God, the Lord our one God.' (Deuteronomy 6: 4). This monotheistic faith (i.e. belief in one God) - which Muslims and Christians claim to share - has shaped Jewish belief and practice, often in situations of conflict and oppression. This faith in the one God, whose will is revealed in the Torah, is the basis for Jewish morality.

- **Love of God and love for one another** is the primary outcome of this faith. 'You must love the Lord your God with all your heart and with all your soul and with all your strength. These commandments I give you this day are to be remembered and taken to heart.' (Deuteronomy 6: 5-6). Jewish morality is, therefore, at least in part a matter of understanding the ethical demands of this commandment to love one another.

- **The covenant** is a fundamental expression and sign of God's love. It takes the form: 'If only you will now listen to me and keep my covenant, then out of all peoples you will become my special possession' (Exodus 19: 5). Three characteristics become clear from this text. Firstly, the covenant is God's initiative; God takes the first step. Secondly, the covenant binds God and God's chosen people. Thirdly, the covenant demands from the Jews obedience to God's law. So living ethically, on the basis of the Torah, is a fundamental requirement of the covenant. Morality is not an optional extra for Jews.

- It is worth repeating here that **the Torah** is not just a written text: the law that it contains is written on the hearts of the Jewish people — it is a matter of faith and belief. It expresses the heart of God's covenant love. Through the Torah and the Talmud Judaism is able to discover the right path (halakhah).

- **The Sabbath** is one of the key and distinctive commandments of Judaism and marks the seventh day of the week as a day of rest. Genesis tells that God rested from creation on the seventh day, but also it was seen as offering a day of rest for slaves and labourers. There are strict laws about keeping the Sabbath and these have implications for Jewish ethics as well as worship.

- **The Exodus experience** of liberation by God from slavery and captivity in Egypt shaped the Jews' understanding of God (God is the Exodus God). They occupied the land of Canaan, promised by God to Abraham, the father of the nation, and they saw themselves as those whom God had freed from captivity and called to be a nation and a people. In the sixth century BCE exile in Babylon meant that Jews relived the experience of Exodus. It was this new experience of oppression that finally led to the definition of Jewish law and morality, the content of Hebrew scriptures and the central affirmations of Jewish faith.

5.5.3 Absolute rules, general principles and personal circumstances

It should be obvious from what has been written about Judaism so far that there is some ambiguity in relation to absolute rules, general principles and personal circumstances. On the one hand, the Torah has an absolute claim on Jews. It is God-given and is the ultimate authority in relation to belief and morality. For many Jews (such as the Hasidim), the Torah, therefore, makes an absolute claim on their lives.

On the other hand, for other Jews, the Torah is authoritative but it does not - in every detail - have an absolute claim on their lives. Rather it contains a series of fundamentally important general principles that have been interpreted over many centuries by many rabbis (including the writings in the Talmud) and that need constant re-interpretation in the light of their contemporary context and personal circumstances.

Norman Solomon[54] says that traditional halakhah 'resists the tendency to moral absolutism' with three exceptions: the worship of idols, committing adultery and the shedding of innocent blood are all prohibited. Jewish morality is, therefore, a matter of balancing ethical obligations rather than fulfilling the demands of the law, regardless of the consequences, according to Norman Solomon.

Tasks

Writing tasks	(a)	Outline what is meant by moral absolutism.
	(b)	Discuss, from the perspective of Judaism, whether there is a place for moral absolutism in today's society.

5.5.4 Reason and conscience

Both reason and conscience have an important place in Jewish ethics. In fact, rabbinical interpretation of the Torah uses logic, reason and debate to come to an understanding of the application of the Torah to a contemporary ethical issue. Such reasoned debate often focuses on a particular topic and seeks to draw more general ethical conclusions from a specific example. This is in contrast to some other traditions of ethical argument that would argue from a more general principle and draw conclusions about the particular case being considered.

The importance that is given to individual conscience in Jewish ethics varies among the traditions. For example, in the ultra-orthodox traditions the emphasis would be on the authoritative claims of the Torah and Talmud. Obedience to the Law would be the ultimate obligation and would always have precedence over personal compassion. Individual conscience could never take precedence over the demands of the Torah in making decisions about morality. On the other hand, in less orthodox traditions there is considerable scope for conscience, even when that seems to be in conflict with the traditional interpretation of the demands of the law. There must always be scope for compassion. Here individual conscience has considerable autonomy.

5.5.5 Diversity

This section on the moral principles of Judaism makes it clear that there is considerable diversity within contemporary Judaism. Crucially, this diversity depends upon the way in which different traditions within Judaism regard the authority of the Torah and consequently the place given to the individual conscience in moral decision-making.

Three examples have been noted: Orthodox Judaism, with its adherence to strict observance of the demands of the Torah in personal, ritual and ethical matters; Conservative Judaism, which allows some flexibility of approach in the light of personal circumstances, but without in any way undermining the authority of the Torah; and Reform Judaism, which gives greater prominence to personal conscience in shaping faith and morality in response to contemporary contexts.

Three key concepts provide unity among these diverse groups. First, all Jews have a strong sense of belonging to the Jewish family, whether in Israel itself or within the worldwide Diaspora (Jewish communities around the world). Second, although different groups have a different attitude to the interpretation of the Torah, all share a fundamental belief that the Torah is the heart of Judaism and regard the Torah as a sacred and authoritative text. Finally, and perhaps most importantly, all Jews share the ancient and distinctive faith in God as the one and only God. The diversity of ethical responses within Judaism must be understood against the background of these common characteristics.

Class discussion

Invite someone from a local synagogue or Jewish community to visit the class:

(a) discuss with them how they respond to Jewish teaching in their own life;

(b) explore with them whether different situations could lead to people having different views on ethical issues, for example, in relation to sexual ethics;

(c) write a short report about your discussions for the school/college magazine.

5.6 Sikhism

Sikhism originated in the Punjab in North-east India, but today there are Sikh communities in many countries around the world, and their leaders often play a prominent role in the life of their wider communities. Sikhism is rooted within the Indian religious traditions, seeks to be tolerant of other faiths and has embraced some aspects of other faiths.

Indarjit Singh quotes these lines from the Sikh scriptures as a summary of the Sikh approach to ethics:

Sikhism has much in common with other Indian religions but has developed its own unique identity.

'Truth is high,
but higher still
is truthful living.'

(Guru Granth Sahib, p. 62)[55]

Chapter 5

5.6.1 Religious texts, traditions and authorities

Texts

Two religious texts are important for Sikhism:

The thoughts of the ten Gurus, contained in the Guru Granth Sahib, are the highest human authority in Sikhism.

- **Guru Granth Sahib:** This is the sacred Scripture of Sikhism (sometimes referred to as Adi Granth) and is regarded with great respect and given a place of honour in the local Gurdwaras (places of worship and meeting). It contains thoughts of the ten Gurus from Guru Nanak (1469-1539CE) to Guru Gobind Singh (1666-1708) in the form of sacred hymns. This collection was itself granted Guru status by Guru Gobind Singh.

- **Rahit Maryada:** This is the most recent code of conduct for Sikhs, agreed in 1945. It offers guidance for the Sikh way of life and Sikhs are able to make decisions about personal and social morality in the light of its guidance.

Authority

There are a number of inter-related aspects of authority within Sikhism:

- Ultimate authority over the life of the universe and over human conduct rests in the one God.

- Gurus are understood not only as teachers but also as holy persons who mediate the divine to human beings. As such they are the highest human authorities.

- The ten Gurus (whose thoughts are gathered in the Guru Granth Sahib) have the highest authority and the greatest significance in the development of Sikhism.

- Local authority for Sikhs is vested in the Khalsa (or local community), inaugurated by Guru Gobal Singh in 1699, which can make a decision which is binding on the local community of Sikhs.

Seminar topic

Discuss the importance of authority in relation to ethics.

'There can be no morality without a religious authority.' Evaluate this view from the perspective of Sikhism.

5.6.2 Religious concepts and moral attitudes

(a) The fundamental responsibility of human beings is to follow the path of God's will, which leads towards truth and goodness. The scriptures of Guru Granth Sahib offer guidance about how this may be achieved. Indarjit Singh[56] suggests three paths that Sikhs should follow which provide the religious and moral framework for the Sikh way of life:

- **Nam japna** (or 'meditation on God'): Meditation on God helps to given human beings a better understanding of the purpose and meaning of life, and a sense of perspective and direction.

The following words appear at the beginning of Guru Granth Sahib:

'There is one God.
Eternal truth is his name;
Maker of all things;
Fearing nothing and at enmity with nothing;
Timeless is his image
Not begotten, being of his own Being;
By his grace made known to humanity,
He was there before time.
He was present in the earliest age.
Is present now
And shall be evermore.'

Indarjit Singh highlights four fundamental outcomes from the passage from Guru Granth Sahib:

- God is one and there is only one God, the God of all humanity, common to all peoples and all religions.

- Since God is 'at enmity with nothing' all persons and nations are equal in God's sight and none receives greater favour than others.

- God is 'not begotten, being of his own Being', 'a permanent presence in an otherwise finite world.'

- Since God is the God of all humanity, there can be only one human family of equals. This has important ethical implications, as we shall see.

Tasks

Writing tasks	'There is one God. Eternal truth is his name; maker of all things; fearing nothing and at enmity with nothing; timeless is his image; not begotten, being of his own Being; by his grace made known to humanity, he was there before time. He was present in the earliest age. Is present now and shall be evermore.'
	Guru Granth Sahib, p.1
	(a) What are the characteristics which Guru Granth Sahib attributes to God?
	(b) What is the relationship between 'meditation on God' and 'seeking the right moral path'?

As the lotus produces a beautiful flower although its roots are in muddy waters, so human beings are called to 'flower' morally within society, despite its meanness and injustice. Hindus see the lotus flower as a religious symbol for beauty and non-attachment while Buddhists see it as a symbol of the true nature of those who float free of ignorance and attain enlightenment.

- **Kirat karna** (or 'earning by one's own efforts'): A holy person is not someone who withdraws from the world for meditation and reflection and so becomes dependent on others for daily needs. Rather a holy person is someone who meditates on God while remaining within society with its challenges and needs. Guru Nanak described this in terms of the lotus flower which has its roots in muddy waters but produces a most beautiful flower. Thus Sikhs 'should live in society, work constantly for its improvement, and yet always be above its meanness and pettiness.'[57]

This understanding of the Sikh obligation to transform society has important ethical and social implications. This leads to the third of the three paths.

- **Vand chakna** (or 'sharing with others'): In one sense, this is an obvious outcome of meditation on God and the life-affirming commitment to changing society. Making one's skills available in service to the community is a fundamental moral obligation.

(b) Two key fundamental moral attitudes are suggested by these religious paths or dimensions:

- **The equality of the human family:** As we have seen, this has considerable importance for Sikhs. For example, Sikhism lays considerable emphasis on equality between women and men (although this noble teaching of the Gurus has not always been reflected in practice). It rejects the Indian caste or class system and works towards abolishing discrimination (for example, on the basis of race, gender or religion). Singh quotes Akal Ustat (86:16) which says:

The Hindus and the Muslims are all one,
Each has the habits of different environments,
But all (people) have the same eyes, the same body,
The same form compounded of the same elements,
They are all one form.
The one Lord made them all.

Thus 'different cultures, different ways of life are not barriers between people, but gateways to a fuller understanding and enrichment of life itself' (Indarjit Singh).[58]

- **Upholding the rights of others:** This is not just a matter of tolerating others and allowing them freedom. It is rather a matter of being committed to making personal sacrifice and effort to uphold and struggle for the rights and equality of others.

Through moral attitudes such as these, Sikhs are encouraged to be positively engaged in the life of society around them. Morality then becomes not just a matter of personal behaviour but a commitment to social action.

Task

Writing task	'Morality is not just a matter of personal behaviour but a commitment to social action.'
	Evaluate this statement from a Sikh perspective.

(c)   Although Sikhism does not include a concept of 'sin' as such, it does recognise that human beings are subject to temptations that hinder spiritual development, namely, lust, anger, greed, undue attachment and pride. The three paths of spiritual development enable human beings to resist the influence of these temptations.

5.6.3 Absolute rules, general principles and personal circumstances

As we have already seen, Sikhism does not offer a set of absolute rules to be obeyed by everyone in all circumstances. The Guru Granth Sahib and the Rahit Maryada are understood as offering reflection and guidance that enables Sikhs to discover the correct path to follow in response to personal circumstances and contemporary situations. Along this path to spiritual and moral development, however, equality and human rights are absolute moral principles.

Class discussion

Invite someone from the local Sikh temple or local community to visit the class:

(a) discuss with them how they respond to Sikh teaching in their own life;

(b) explore with them whether different circumstances and situations could lead to different views on moral issues; for example, in relation to sexual ethics;

(c) write a brief report of your discussion for the school/college newspaper.

5.6.4/5.6.5 Reason, conscience and diversity

We can conclude from what has been written above that:

- Sikhs regard Guru Granth Sahib and the Rahit Maryada as authoritative and are encouraged to use human reason to interpret these texts;

- there is a place for freedom of conscience in making ethical decisions in the light of these texts;

- while there is diversity within Sikhism partly as the result of historical reforms and partly because of different local contexts, the above texts provide unity;

- since God is one, the diverse ways of knowing God in different religions are equally valid;

- these attitudes are fundamental to Sikh ethics at a particular time and place.

Texts, traditions and authority

Buddhism
Ethics based on dharma (teaching), contained in Pali Canon, the written form of the oral teaching of Buddha. Offered as guidance not as final authority.

Christianity
Texts of Hebrew Scriptures and New Testament. Life and teaching of Jesus. Authority of Church. Authority of Scripture.

Hinduism
Range of scriptures: Vedas, Upanishads, Dharmashatras, Bhagavat Gita. Diverse traditions: Shivaism, Vishnuism, Saktism.

What are the central texts of the world religions?
What are their main religious traditions?
Where are the main sources of moral authority?

Islam
Ultimate authority: will of Allah recorded in Qur'an. Hadith: sayings of Muhammad. Together these form the basis of Shari'ah Law.

Judaism
Based on Torah (Pentateuch) including Decalogue. Talmud (600CE): rules and traditions. Basis of halakah: right path.

Sikhism
God is the ultimate authority. Highest human authority: thoughts of the 10 gurus in Guru Granth Sahib & Rihat Maryada: summary of Sikh way of life.

Religious concepts and moral attitudes

Buddhism
Karma
Three marks of existence
Five precepts
Four Noble Truths
Eightfold Path

Christianity
Faith in Triune God
Human beings as sinful
Centrality of love (agape)
The kingdom of God

Hinduism
Dharma (duty)
Varna (class)
Ashramas (four stages of life)
Karma (action or force towards rebirth)

What are the key religious concepts of the world religions?
What are their main moral attitudes?

Islam
Allah (God) is one
Holistic guidance
Accountability to God
Balance, Peace
Five pillars of Islam

Judaism
God is one Lord
Love of God and each other
The Covenant
The Sabbath
The Exodus experience

Sikhism
Meditation on God (Nam japna)
Earning by own efforts (Kirat karna)
Sharing with others (Vand chakna)
Human Equality
Human Rights

Absolute rules, general principles and personal circumstances

Buddhism
No absolute rules; general principles are offered as guidance for those seeking enlightenment, to be used or rejected as appropriate.

Christianity
Some: Christian ethics as a set of absolute rules. Others: a way of life founded on love (agape).

Hinduism
Dharma as cosmic principle. Moral behaviour appropriate to caste and ashrama rather than absolute rules.

Does the religion offer an absolute morality
or
does it allow personal circumstances and local context to be taken into consideration?

Islam
Generally, Shari'ah Law, based on God's will, is absolute. Defence of Islam must take precedence over freedom of the individual.

Judaism
Laws and rules of Torah and Talmud are not arbitrary; they have the authority of God: only the text is infallible.

Sikhism
Rihat Maryada authoritative but not absolute. Oneness of human family and tolerance are paramount.

Role of reason and conscience

Buddhism
Considerable flexibility in ways of following teachings. Teachings must be tested by personal experience, wisdom and conscience.

Christianity
Place for conscience in relation to authority of Bible and Church. Divergence in scope for reason (see Natural Law).

Hinduism
Whereas written sources are important, appropriate behaviour within class or ashrama is the key. Conscience is final arbiter.

What is the place of God-given conscience and human reason in relation to ethical precepts?

Islam
Some scope for personal choice based on diverse understandings of Shari'ah.

Judaism
Mainly based on Torah but reason and conscience have part to play: 'Torah…deserves the subtlety of human ingenuity' to interpret it.'

Sikhism
Freedom from conscience to decide questions of conduct in light of codes of practice based on Guru Granth Sahib and Rihat Maryada.

Ethical diversity

Buddhism
Diversity of traditions: e.g. Theravada & Mahayana. Diversity of personal responses in different situations.

Christianity
Diversity between Bible-based and church/tradition centred ethics. Diversity on issues e.g. war, sexual ethics, public ethics.

Hinduism
Diversity of forms of God. Diversity of scriptures and traditions. Diverse duties and rights according to class etc.

How much scope is there for diversity in developing moral attitudes?

Islam
Some scope for diversity on ethical matters. Four schools, based on work of four Imams: Malik, Hanafi, Shafi, Hanbal.

Judaism
Diversity is result of disagreement on interpretation of Torah between Orthodox, Conservative, Reform and Liberal Jews.

Sikhism
Diversity within the worldwide Sikh community is largely the result of living in different social contexts especially outside India.

Glossary

precepts	ideas or concepts
religious authorities	individuals or bodies that have the power to make decisions about the life and conduct of a particular religion or religious organisation
religious texts	writings which are central to particular religions (e.g. the Hebrew Scriptures)
religious traditions	beliefs, rites and practices which have been handed on across the centuries within a particular religion

Section 5.1

connectedness	the belief that human beings are inter-related to one another and to the natural world
doctrine	a religion's body of teaching on matters of faith and belief
Sanskrit literature	writings in the ancient language of Buddhism (and Hinduism) in India
the historical Buddha	the Buddha as he existed at a given time and period of history

Section 5.2

autonomy / autonomous	freedom to act according to one's own understanding or conscience
Ecumenical Councils	meetings of bishops and archbishops in the ancient Church which made authoritative decisions about the doctrine and life of the Church
Great Schism	the historic division between the Western Church and the Eastern Church in 1054CE which led to the Roman Catholic Church and the Orthodox Churches respectively
Hebrew people	another name for the Jews, the people who spoke - and still speak - the Hebrew language
Pharisee	religious Jews in the time of Jesus who held a very strict understanding of the Jewish law
synagogue	the building in which Jews meet for worship and teaching
the Gospels	literally meaning 'good news', this is the term used to describe the first four 'books' of the New Testament, the Gospels of Matthew, Mark, Luke and John

Section 5.3

canonical	an approved collection of religious texts or writings
embodied	literally, to take bodily form in
epics	traditional, often mythical, stories
ethical relativism	a moral position which depends on the particular situation rather than on a predetermined rule or law
hierarchical	a social structure which resembles a pyramid, with those who have the greatest significance, status and authority at the top (or apex) of the pyramid
reincarnation	a cycle of birth and rebirth from one life to the next

Section 5.4

Allah	Arabic term for God
imam	cleric who leads prayers in a mosque

Section 5.5

covenant	a binding agreement between two parties of which there are a number of examples in the Hebrew Scriptures e.g. the covenant with Abraham and the covenant with Moses
liturgy	patterns or orders of worship
rabbi/rabbinical	a Jewish teacher of the law/relating to or derived from a rabbi

Section 5.6

begotten	born of a parent or parents
mediate	to act as channels of (the divine)

World Religions and Ethical Theories

After studying this chapter you should be able to determine the degree of compatibility between the three ethical theories studied in chapters 2-4 and the traditional ethical teaching of the one major world religion you have selected for study.

This chapter does not attempt to offer definitive answers to questions of compatibility. The individual and group tasks will encourage you to explore the connections between the theories and the religious teachings, in relation to contemporary moral issues, so that you can draw your own conclusions.

Introduction

Before exploring the degree of compatibility between the major world religions and the three ethical theories already studied, it will be helpful to be reminded of the key principles of these theories.

- **Natural Law** may be summarised as follows:

  - there is a God-given design and purpose within the natural world;

  - this design and purpose can be discerned by human reason;

  - through human reason, therefore, human beings can understand the moral principles which are inherent within creation;

  - the goal of moral or ethical action is to achieve 'the highest good';

  - in the process of deciding on the appropriate ethical action, a distinction needs to be drawn between 'efficient cause' (the pragmatic explanation for an action or event or situation) and the 'final cause' (the ultimate meaning and purpose of an event);

  - by applying these principles Natural Law seeks to establish moral principles which have an absolute claim on human beings, irrespective of the consequences of an act or of particular personal circumstances.

- **Utilitarianism** may be summarised as follows:

  - it is based on utility or usefulness;

  - its central principle is 'the greatest happiness for the greatest number';

  - happiness (or its opposite, pain) may be measured by applying 'the hedonic calculus';

  - put at its simplest, it does not ask 'Is this action right or wrong in itself?' but rather 'Is the consequence of this act right or wrong, ethically acceptable or not?';

❑ two forms of Utilitarianism can be distinguished:

act Utilitarianism asks 'what acts lead to the greatest happiness?' and seeks to develop ethical rules based on the responses;

rule Utilitarianism asks 'what rules should be followed?' and seeks to define what actions would be morally acceptable on the basis of these rules.

- **Situation Ethics** may be summarised as follows:

  ❑ it rejects absolute moral rules that are to be applied in every situation;

  ❑ it insists that there is only one absolute rule, the law of love;

  ❑ in every situation, therefore, the right thing to do is what love demands;

  ❑ it is based on six fundamental principles:

   - *only love is intrinsically good;*

   - *love is the ruling norm;*

   - *love and justice are the same;*

   - *love always wills the neighbour's good;*

   - *only the end justifies the means;*

   - *love's decisions are made situationally.*

  ❑ it also works with four working principles:

   - *pragmatism;*

   - *relativism;*

   - *positivism;*

   - *personalism.*

We must now ask: To what extent are the traditional ethical principles of the major world religions compatible with these ethical theories?
The following sections on the six world religions set out some key principles and approaches, which are discussed more fully in the previous chapter. Students are invited to explore for themselves, through a range of individual and group tasks, whether or not a particular religion is compatible with Natural Law, Utilitarianism and Situation Ethics.

6.1   Buddhism

6.1.1 Natural Law:

(a) At the heart of Buddhism is the teaching of the Buddha, and the interpretation and application of that teaching throughout the centuries in a range of different contexts. The Buddha offered his teaching, not as an absolute set of rules, but rather as ethical and spiritual principles to be followed if they were considered helpful, or to be set aside if they were considered unhelpful to a particular person in a particular situation.

(b) The goal of Buddhism is to enable human beings to achieve spiritual and moral enlightenment.

(c) Fundamentally, Buddhism offers guidelines for spiritual and ethical development, for which the Buddha is a model to follow, rather than a theological framework founded on a transcendent being who gives the universe a purpose and meaning.

(d) Buddhism lays considerable emphasis on individual responsibility for moral action: 'In the end, individuals are responsible for their actions and have an obligation to test the tradition by their own experience.'[59]

(e) Buddhism emphasises connectedness between human beings and one another, and between human beings and the natural world, as an important aspect of the design and purpose of the universe.

6.1.2 Utilitarianism

(a) Buddhism teaches that all ethically significant actions (karma) have their consequences:
'What you do today will determine the kind of person you become tomorrow'.

(b) Buddhism also teaches that at the heart of spiritual and ethical development is the need to determine the motivation or intention behind actions ('It is choice or intention that I call karma').

(c) In Buddhist understanding, one of the marks of the human condition (dukkha) is that perfect happiness is not possible, 'happiness is never permanent, all happiness is tainted'.

<table>
<tr><td>*Class discussion*</td></tr>
<tr><td>*In the light of these fundamental approaches to ethical decision-making, determine how far Buddhism is compatible with Natural Law?*</td></tr>
</table>

Task

<table>
<tr><td>**Writing task**</td><td>'The Buddhist ethical and spiritual path [can be described] as a form of …Utilitarianism…It is distinctly consequentialist.'[60]

Evaluate this view.</td></tr>
</table>

6.1.3 Situation Ethics

(a) Buddhism rejects the idea of absolute ethical rules that apply to everyone in every situation.

(b) Buddhism seeks to overcome hate, greed and ignorance and offers a path towards compassion, gentleness and serenity.

(c) Within Buddhism right action must be worked out according to the time, place and situation in which people find themselves.

(d)   'A basic pragmatism underlines all Buddhist teaching'.

(e)   'At the heart of Buddhism there are the socially motivating qualities of 'simple compassion' and 'sympathy'.[61]

Task

Writing task	Evaluate the compatibility between these Buddhist approaches, and the six fundamental principles and four working principles of Situation Ethics.

6.2   Christianity

6.2.1 Natural Law

(a)   Although rooted in Aristotle's secular (non-religious) philosophy, Natural Law was developed by the Catholic theologian and moralist, Thomas Aquinas, who used the secular philosophy as a basis for a Christian morality.

(b)   Christianity has at its heart the belief that God created the universe, giving it a design and a purpose, and that human beings, created 'in the image of God', are able to discern God's will by the use of human reason.

(c)   Some Churches and Christian moralists claim that Natural Law and Biblical commandments (e.g. in the Ten Commandments and in Jesus' teaching) can be brought together to produce an absolutist ethical code. Others claim that Biblical authority must always have precedence over Natural Law in relation to Christian ethics.

(d)   When a rich young man asked Jesus, 'Teacher, what good deed must I do to have eternal life?' Jesus answered '…If you wish to enter into life, keep the commandments…You shall not murder; You shall not commit adultery; You shall not steal…' (Matthew 19: 16 ff.). Christianity, therefore, can be thought of as offering absolute ethical rules to enable human beings to attain 'the highest good' of love.

Class discussion

'[Statements by the Popes of the Roman Catholic Church] simply assume the validity of Natural Law and draw upon it to provide a philosophical framework within which they can speak about particularly troubling moral and social issues.'[62]

Is a modern understanding of Christian morality consistent with the traditional Natural Law theory?

6.2.2 Utilitarianism

(a)   Mill believed that Utilitarianism had caught the spirit of the Golden Rule (namely, 'do to others what you would want them to do to you') by proposing the principle of 'the greatest happiness for the greatest number'.

(b)   Historically, Utilitarianism made a major contribution to social reform, on the basis of justice and equality and, in this sense, shared many of the goals of Christian social reformers.

(c)   The concept of beatitude (blessedness) is translated by the Good News Bible as 'Happy are they...' in Matthew 5: 1-12. This suggests that the idea of happiness, as defined by Utilitarianism, could be compatible with the spiritual and moral goals of Christian living.

(d)   On the other hand, hedonism (i.e. life seen as nothing but the pursuit of pleasure or happiness) is considered to be inconsistent with Christian ethics, which has the pursuit of love rather than happiness at its heart.

(e)   Love, compassion, equality and generosity could be defined as core Christian values. Such values were emphasised in Mill's re-interpretation of Utilitarianism as being of greater moral worth.

(f)   Some Christians believe that there are some acts which are wrong in themselves irrespective of their consequences for other people e.g. it is always wrong to murder.

Task

Writing task	'Utilitarianism has caught the spirit of the Golden Rule, namely, "do to others what you would want others to do to you" '. Evaluate this view from the perspective of Christianity.

6.2.3 Situation Ethics

(a) Situation Ethics was developed by Fletcher as a specific attempt to set out a contemporary framework for Christian Ethics.

(b) Jesus taught that love to God and to neighbours is the heart of Christian living and morality. The founding principle of Situation Ethics is that there is only one absolute law, namely, the law of love. In any situation the question to be asked is, 'What is the demand of the law of love?'

(c) Traditionally, Christianity teaches that there is a fundamental moral law which is based on the Ten Commandments and the teaching of Jesus, and which remains valid for everyone at all times and in all places. Many Christians would claim that this moral clarity and authority is needed today, particularly in our secular Western society.

(d) On the other hand, Christian leaders such as Bishop Spong in the USA, claim that it is necessary to transform the assumptions of traditional Christian ethics. 'One cannot speak [clearly] to the ethical concerns of this generation by quoting two-thousand- to four-thousand-year-old authorities who claim to represent God's final word on [ethical subjects].'[63]

Task

Writing tasks	Bishop John Spong claims[64] that Christian ethics is not about controlling behaviour but about embracing 'the fullness of life', that is, inviting people to live their life as fully as God desires (see The Gospel of John, chapter 10, verse 10).
	(a) Outline what Situation Ethics understands by 'the law of love'.
	(b) Explain how Situation Ethics contributes to an understanding of Christian ethics as a way of embracing 'fullness of life'.

6.3   Hinduism

6.3.1 Natural Law

(a) Hinduism embraces belief in an eternal cosmic creative force, God or Brahma, which takes many forms.

(b) Hinduism sees human beings not as isolated individuals but as part of the cosmic whole, living in harmony with all things.

(c) Hinduism lays considerable emphasis on the obligation to fulfil one's duties and responsibilities as determined by birth.

(d) Dharma provides a form or structure of laws and regulations that become binding within particular cultures, as well as an ethical framework for behaviour.

(e) Dharma is predominantly concerned with the attainment of purity or the ultimate good, which is the most desired state of being.

(f) Hinduism emphasises individual conscience in relation to dharma and, therefore, allows for considerable diversity in the way in which dharma is applied in different situations, times and personal circumstances.

6.3.2 Utilitarianism

(a) Hindu dharma provides a ritual and ethical basis for a cycle of reincarnation and salvation on the path towards unity.

(b) Hindu karma stresses the importance of right action, the right motivation for action and the consequences of actions, not only in this life but over several lifetimes.

(c) The ethic of a householder stresses three goals of life or three paths, namely, fulfilling social and moral obligations (dharma), becoming prosperous, and the experience of pleasure.

(d) The strong sense of the inter-relatedness of human beings within Hinduism means that ethical behaviour takes on a strong social dimension, in which the good of others has a central place.

Class discussion

'While supreme authority rests in an invisible creative force, sometimes called God or Brahma... the ultimate guide for an individual believer is his or her conscience.'

In the light of this view, discuss whether or not Hinduism is compatible with the principles of Natural Law.

Task

Writing task	'Hinduism's emphasis on the consequences of one's actions, not only in this life but also in future lifetimes indicates that it is a strongly utilitarian religion.' Evaluate this view.

6.3.3 Situation Ethics

(a) Hinduism stresses the centrality of individual conscience, which asks in each situation, 'what is appropriate behaviour in these particular circumstances?'

(b) The absolute demand of Hinduism is the obligation to fulfil one's duty according to caste and stage of life.

(c) Hindu ethical approaches are fundamentally situational.

(d) Balance and harmony between the individual, other human beings and the whole created order, provides a framework for Hindu morality.

   (e)   Gita offers a model of an ethical person who is 'without hatred of any creature, friendly and compassionate…' (Gita 12.13)[65]

Tasks

Writing tasks	(a)	Evaluate the compatibility between these Hindu approaches, and the six fundamental principles and four working principles of Situation Ethics.
	(b)	Determine whether Natural Law, Utilitarianism or Situation Ethics is most compatible with Hindu ethical teaching.

6.4   Islam

(a)   Belief in Allah, who is One, is fundamental to Islam.

(b)   The will of Allah determines everything in the universe. Ethics are understood as conduct by which human beings submit in a natural way to God's purpose within the universe.

(c)   The final will and purpose of God was revealed to the prophet Muhammad and recorded in the Qur'an. The acts and saying of Muhammad are recorded in the Hadith. Shari'ah law, which is the basis of Islamic ethics, is based on these authoritative texts.

(d)   Islam is understood as God's straight path which people must follow in all aspects of their lives.

(e)   The teaching of Islam has an absolute claim on the life and conduct of Muslims at all times and in all situations.

(f)   Applying this absolute teaching calls for the use of human reason and reflection.

(g)   Balance, for example, between justice and compassion, is an important principle of Islamic ethics.

Class discussion

In the light of these fundamental approaches to ethical decision-making, discuss whether Natural Law, Utilitarianism or Situation Ethics is most compatible with Islamic ethics.

6.5   Judaism

(a)   Judaism has a fundamental belief in one God, Creator, Designer and Sustainer of the universe.

(b)   The Torah is understood as the ultimate and authoritative will of God, given by God to enable human beings to achieve their divine purpose.

(c)   Reasoned argument and debate play a very important part in interpreting the ethical implication of the teaching of the Torah, but some would question whether

Jewish morality is fundamentally rational, preferring to believe that Jewish law has been revealed by God.

(d) Some Orthodox traditions within Judaism believe that the Torah has an absolute claim on the individual and has to be obeyed, even if personal compassion or individual conscience calls for a different response.

(e) Other traditions within Judaism believe that there has to be a flexible approach to obedience to the law, in the light of conscience or personal or social circumstances. They therefore commend a more pragmatic approach, which lays more emphasis on the consequences of an action than on the absolute demands of the Torah.

Class discussion

In the light of these observations, determine whether Natural Law, Utilitarianism or Situation Ethics is most compatible with Jewish ethics.

6.6   Sikhism

(a) The God who is one is the ultimate authority in the universe and in the life of human beings; meditation on God and following the right path must go hand in hand.

(b) The Gurus mediate the divine to human beings.

(c) The teaching of the ten Gurus in the Guru Granth Sahib is offered not as a set of absolute rules for moral conduct, but as guidance in the search for truth and goodness.

(d) Sikh morality is not just a matter of personal behaviour but a commitment to seek the greater good of the community, on the basis of equality, tolerance and human rights.

(e) Sikh ethics do not attempt to set out ethical rules, to be applied to everyone in every situation, but offer help in making moral decisions in different situations and personal circumstances.

Tasks

Writing tasks	(a) Outline the main principles of Utilitarianism.
	(b) Determine the degree to which Utilitarianism is compatible with the ethical approach of Sikhism.

Buddhism and ethical theories

Buddhism is primarily a set of practical, moral and spiritual guidelines, in the context of birth and rebirth, rather than belief in a transcendent God. Buddhism would not normally subscribe to a **Natural Law** based on a 'divine' cosmic purpose.

Buddhists believe that all ethically significant actions (karma) have their consequences: 'What you do today will determine the sort of person you become tomorrow.' In this sense, there is a compatibility with **Utilitarianism**.

What degree of compatibility exists between Buddhism and the three ethical theories?

Buddhism is a path (not a set of commandments) towards compassion, gentleness and serenity, and to overcome hate, greed and ignorance. So it could be seen as being compatible with **Situation Ethics**.

Christianity and ethical theories

In Catholic tradition **Natural Law** and the use of reason was and continues to be, a fundamental basis for morality. The Reformation tradition sets the Bible under the guidance of the Spirit as the highest authority for morality.

Utilitarianism, developed within a Christian context but not openly Christian in its concepts, would be affirmed by some for its emphasis on highest good and equality, but criticised by others for its emphasis on consequences.

What degree of compatibility exists between Christianity and the three ethical theories?

Situation Ethics as a contemporary ethic based on teaching of Jesus that the law of love (agape) is absolute would be embraced by some. Others would criticise its lack of moral clarity and authority.

Hinduism and ethical theories

Hinduism is characteristically diverse in belief and practice, so it would reject the **Natural Law** attempt to set out a universally applicable law. But Hindu belief that humanity is vitally linked with the created world leads to an ethical approach based on harmony.

The Hindu concept of dharma emphasizes each individual's duty 'to act in such a way that righteousness is achieved. Hindus therefore ask: 'How must I act to achieve this?' In this sense, there may be some compatibility between Hinduism and act **Utilitarianism**.

What degree of compatibility exists between Hinduism and the three ethical theories?

Hinduism allows for flexibility of approaches to achieving dharma and sees balance and harmony as goals of human life. So there may be compatibility between this contextual and harmonic approach and **Situation Ethics**.

Islam and ethical theories

Shari'ah Law, derived from Qur'an and Hadith is a **Natural Law** created by Allah which determines everything in the universe and sets out laws for a whole way of life founded on the Islamic faith.

Generally, the absolutism of Islam would be considered to be incompatible with the emphasis of **Utilitarianism** on consequences rather than on universally applicable moral laws.

What degree of compatibility exists between Islam and the three ethical theories?

Situation Ethics, with its emphasis on the law of love as the only absolute and its contextual approach to morality, would be incompatible with Islam.

Judaism and ethical theories

Judaism believes that in creating the universe God gave it purpose and design and gave human beings a set of commandments (in the Torah) which are binding on God's people. So Judaism could be seen as compatible with **Natural Law**.

Judaism's emphasis is on a faithful obedience to a set of commandments and rules which are universally applicable. **Utilitarianism's** emphasis on consequences and seeking the greater happiness for the greatest number would be of secondary importance.

What degree of compatibility exists between Judaism and the three ethical theories?

On the one hand, the love of God is at the heart of the Torah. On the other hand, it offers laws which make an absolute claim on Jews. So while the claim of love is common to both, the contextual nature of **Situation Ethics** is incompatible.

Sikhism and ethical theories

Sikhism teaches that those who move in the direction of God's will (hukam) will be turned towards truth and goodness. This is achieved by meditation or reflection on eternal truths. These three aspects reflect the central principles of **Natural law**.

While Sikhism is unlikely to embrace the consequential approach of **Utilitarianism**, its emphasis on the oneness of the human family, equality and tolerance for all could be seen as compatible with 'the greater happiness for the greatest number.'

What degree of compatibility exists between Sikhism and the three ethical theories?

Sikhism's emphasis on a life of prayer, free from self-centredness and dedicated to the service of others, and the absence of 'thou shalt', could be seen as compatible with the centrality of the law of love in **Situation Ethics**.

Glossary

compatibility   the ability to co-exist

Section 2

Aim of the section

This section focuses on three aspects of Sexual Relationships, namely:

- *marriage, adultery and divorce*
- *sex before marriage*
- *homosexuality*

You are asked to study these aspects from the perspective of one major world religion. You are also expected to be able to demonstrate how ethical decisions can be made, by applying to these three topics the principles of the three ethical theories that you have studied in chapters 2 - 4 above.

Chapters 7, 8 and 9 focus on the three topics and provide opportunities for you to study them from the perspective of your chosen religion. Chapter 10 examines sexual ethics from the perspective of the moral theories studied in Section 1.

Summary diagrams are included in this section. They do not say everything there is to be said, but sum up the main ethical responses in relation to each topic. Remember these charts do not provide all the information you need - fuller information is provided in the text of each chapter.

Marriage, Adultery and Divorce

Aim

After studying this chapter you should be able to understand

- *the ways in which different world religions approach marriage;*

- *the purpose of marriage from religious perspectives;*

- *ethical issues raised by adultery; and*

- *religious attitudes towards divorce and remarriage.*

All religions regard marriage with the utmost seriousness. Marriage is not just a matter of a loving relationship between a man and a woman which is recognised by law. All religions also regard marriage as a basic unit of society.

How does a religious marriage ceremony change the way people understand marriage?

Approaches to marriage

Religions display a range of approaches to marriage:

- Marriage is the norm for most religions but for some religions (e.g. Islam) marriage is a religious requirement and failure to marry is regarded very seriously. At the same time, there is in some religions, such as Buddhism and Christianity, a long and significant tradition of celibacy (that is, a religious commitment not to marry and to refrain from any sexual relationships) among priests and monastic communities.

- Marriage is understood as a divine covenant or sacrament within some religions (e.g. Christianity and Hinduism). A divine covenant is a relationship sealed by God and founded on God's relationship with, and promise to, human beings.

A sacrament is an outward and visible sign of God's will, purpose and gift in the lives of human beings. So when marriage is understood as a divine covenant or a sacrament, it becomes a sacred relationship. Such a view is usually reflected in the religious ceremonies which solemnise and celebrate the marriage.

- In all religions, the ideal is that marriage should be a life-long partnership. Some religions find it easier than others to cope with the possibility that sometimes marriages break down, and recognise that the best interests of all those concerned are best served by ending the marriage.

- Marriage does not only have a religious significance, it is also a social contract i.e. it is recognised legally as a relationship between two people which has legal and social implications in terms of their children, their money, their property etc.

- Marriage may be the consequence of two people who love each other deciding to make a marriage commitment to each other, but in some religions there is also a tradition that decisions about who a person marries are arranged or assisted by the family. Often the balance between these approaches within a particular religion depends on the cultural norms and expectations of the society in which the people concerned live.

- Most religions regard monogamous marriage (i.e. the marriage of one husband to one wife) as the norm, whereas others (e.g. Islam) condone polygamy (i.e. the marriage of one husband to more than one wife) under certain circumstances. But in all situations religions recognise that the law of the land must be upheld.

Seminar topic
Summarise the attitude of your chosen world religion to the approaches to marriage outlined above.

Task

Writing task	'Marriage is an outdated institution. Basing a modern approach to marriage on ancient religious traditions is no longer acceptable.' Evaluate this view from the perspective of one major world religion.

The purpose of marriage

For most religions the purpose of marriage would include the following:

- Marriage establishes a loving, committed and stable relationship between a man and a woman.

- Marriage is a partnership of mutual affection, respect, support and help.

- Marriage provides a moral framework for sexual relationships between a man and a woman.

- The main purpose of marriage is the procreation and nurture of children.

- The family unit, focussed on marriage, provides the best context for the nurture of children in a religious faith.

One example of a religious understanding of the purpose of marriage is found in the Catechism of the Catholic Church (paras. 2364 and 2366):

'(Marriage) is the intimate partnership of life and love established by the Creator and governed by his laws... (The married couple) give themselves totally to one another. They are no longer two; from now on they are one flesh... Fecundity (i.e. being fertile and producing children) is a gift of marriage...Union and procreation are both inherent to the marriage act.'

Another example is found in Sikhism and in the words of Guru Amar Das:

'They are not husband and wife
who only dwell together.
Only they who have one spirit in two bodies
can be called husband and wife.'

Adi Granth: 788

Adultery

Adultery is against the moral law of all the major world religions because:

- it denies the sacramental nature of marriage;

- it undermines the sanctity of marriage;

- it breaks the marriage promises;

- it threatens the family as a cornerstone of society;

- it is a sign of promiscuity and lust.

In some religions there is a specific prohibition on adultery within a sacred text. For example, Judaism and Christianity share the Ten Commandments (see Exodus 20: 1-17), which states:

'You shall not commit adultery'.

Jesus' teaching went even further:

'You have heard that it was said, 'You shall not commit adultery.' But I say to you that every one who looks at a woman lustfully has already committed adultery with her in his heart.'

Matthew 5: 27-28

Similarly, many Buddhists would regard the third precept ('I undertake the rule of training to refrain from the misuse of the senses') as an undertaking not to commit

Class discussion

What are the ethical differences between a religious marriage and a secular marriage?

adultery and believe that hurting a marriage partner by such unfaithfulness is inconsistent with the marriage bond.

Class discussion

Is adultery immoral if there is genuine love?

Divorce

Religions do recognise that marriage relationships do break down. The mutual affections of the marriage partners may change. They may come to recognise that they are incompatible with each other for personal, cultural, social or religious reasons. Sometimes there has been unfaithfulness by one of the partners. In other marriages there may have been cruelty and violence or a failure of mutual support and help.

No religion encourages or welcomes divorce in these circumstances, but nevertheless they recognise, in varying degrees, that divorce may be the only alternative available when marriage breakdown seems beyond reconciliation. In such circumstances, most religions would have the following concerns in mind:

- Divorce must be a last resort when all else has failed.

- Any divorce agreement must make every effort to ensure that any children born within the marriage are nurtured and cared for in their best interests.

Some sacred texts and traditions, however, prohibit divorce except under very restricted conditions. For example, the Christian New Testament prohibits divorce except for 'unchastity'. Jesus said:

'...what I tell you is this: If a man divorces his wife for any cause other than unchastity he involves her in adultery; and whoever marries her commits adultery.'

Matthew 5: 32

On this basis some Christian traditions, such as the Roman Catholic Church, oppose divorce except under very narrowly defined circumstances, such as the marriage being unconsummated (i.e. no sexual intercourse has occurred between the partners):

'Divorce is a grave offence against Natural Law...it does injury to the covenant of salvation, of which sacramental marriage is a sign.'

Catechism, para. 2384

But this position does distinguish between the innocent party who has tried to be faithful to the marriage vow and the unfaithful party. At the same time, the Catechism recognises that under certain circumstances divorce may not be a moral offence:

> 'If civil divorce remains the only possible way of ensuring certain legal rights, the care of the children, or the protection of inheritance, it can be tolerated and does not constitute a moral offence.'
>
> Catechism, para. 2383

Others would argue that, although there is this textual prohibition on divorce, sometimes circumstances mean that the requirements of love, compassion, respect, dignity and care of the children are best served by divorce. Such Christian traditions would find it easier to condone divorce.

This ambivalence (holding opposing attitudes at the same time) over the place of sacred text and the pressures of social and cultural changes affect the ethical stances of many religions on this issue. For example, there is considerable debate within Hinduism about whether marriage breakdown should be grounds for divorce. The sacramental understanding of marriage within Hinduism - especially among high caste Hindus - makes it very difficult to approve of divorce. So in some cultures, (for example, within India itself), this is a very controversial issue, while in other settings, where the legal situation is different (for example, in Britain), the attitudes are inevitably different.

The Islamic Hadith states clearly that, 'Divorce is the most detestable in the sight of God of all permitted things' (Abu Dawud 2173). A number of conditions under which divorce is permitted are laid down. For example, long absence of the husband without knowing his whereabouts, or desertion or moral laxity on the part of either party, are legal grounds for divorce. Divorce can take three forms: by the husband, by the wife, or through the decision of the court.

The question of remarriage of divorced persons is also a difficult issue for religions. For example, those Christian traditions that prohibit divorce find it equally impossible to marry divorced persons, while those Christian traditions that are prepared to condone divorce are usually prepared to remarry divorced persons.

Similarly, while divorce is always the last resort for Muslims, those who have been divorced are free and, indeed, encouraged, to remarry.

Seminar topic

In January 2001 the UK government announced its intention to abandon parts of the Family Law Act 1996. This had allowed divorce without having to name any fault (such as adultery) and encouraged everybody seeking divorce to go through a conciliation process, which would provide the possibility of second thoughts in the hope of saving marriages. It was claimed that the conciliation process had proved unworkable.

The Bishop of Winchester commented: 'I regret that these provisions have proved unworkable and hope that the government will return to these questions very quickly so that family mediation could be offered to everyone.'

continued over

The Lord Chancellor, who is responsible for the legal system on behalf of the government, commented: 'The government is committed to supporting marriage and to supporting families when relationships fail, especially when there are children involved.'

- Use one of the news pages on the Internet (e.g. http://news.bbc.co.uk) to find further information about these and other changes to UK divorce law.

- Discuss whether conciliation and/or family mediation should be a requirement before proceeding to divorce.

- Discuss whether a no fault divorce (that is, a divorce granted by the courts without having to provide evidence that one or other partner has been, for example, unfaithful or cruel or violent) would be a welcome or an unwelcome development.

Task

Writing task	'Divorce is too easy in British society today.' Examine this view from the perspective of one major world religion.

Glossary

adultery	a sexual relationship between a married person and someone who is not his or her husband/wife
Catechism	a summary (or sometimes a longer collection) of religious teaching on matters of faith and morals, often used to instruct new believers. A term which is widely used by the Roman Catholic Church.
conciliation	see **reconciliation**
divine covenant	a binding relationship initiated by God
reconciliation	repairing a broken relationship or re-uniting two people who have been apart (the process is sometimes called 'a conciliation process' or '**mediation**')
sacrament	an outward sign of an inward God-given grace
sanctity of marriage	marriage as a holy or sacred relationship
secular marriage	a marriage which has been solemnised in a non-religious ceremony

Sex before Marriage

Aim

After studying this chapter you should be able to

- *discuss the purpose of sex and sexual intercourse;*

- *understand how sex and human relationships are interconnected;*

- *explore whether marriage is the only framework for sexual relationships.*

The purpose of sex

The following are among the most important purposes of sex:

- it is the ultimate physical expression of mutual love and affection between a man and a woman;

- it is a sign of love and the final seal or bond of a loving commitment;

- it is the means of the procreation of children;

- it enables a man and a woman to have mutual pleasure in one another.

> **Class discussion**
>
> *Do you agree that these are the important purposes of sex? Which is the most important? Which is the least important?*

Sex and human relationships

Most religions would agree that sex must be understood within the context of human relationships. Sexual intercourse can be properly understood only when it is seen not just as a physical act but also as an act which finds its meaning within a relationship of love.

But they would also agree that mutual love and affection are not an adequate basis for sexual intercourse. Marriage, which expresses a loving commitment between a man and a woman, is believed to be the only relationship within which sexual intercourse is morally permissible.

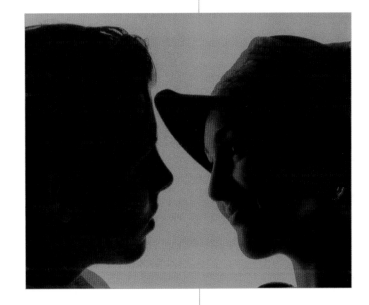

Task

Writing task	'Marriage, which is a loving commitment between a man and a woman, is the only relationship within which sexual intercourse is morally permissible.' Evaluate this view from the perspective of one major world religion.

Religious leaders have been particularly concerned about the rise in casual and pre-marital sex in the UK in recent decades. They see this as to some extent due to the easy availability of contraception. Their concern arises from their belief that such behaviour is against the moral principles of traditional religions, and because such an approach to sex focuses on the satisfaction of physical feelings rather than on sex as a sign of mutual love and commitment.

In Judaism, for example, sexual intercourse is understood within the context of a marriage relationship and so sex outside marriage threatens the highest qualities in human relationships; it robs the sexual act of its true purpose and fails to treat other people with respect.

Similarly, in Sikhism there is a basic emphasis on the importance of family responsibility and self-restraint. Sexual activity is, therefore, ethically acceptable only within marriage and sex before or outside marriage is condemned.

However, recent research by Professor J. Leslie Francis of the University of Wales, Bangor (published by the Welsh National Centre for Religious Education in March 2001)[66] suggests that young people within religious traditions in the UK do not necessarily share the views of religious leaders. For example, only 15% of young Catholics accept their Church's teaching that sex outside marriage is immoral, whereas 49% of young Muslims accept Islamic teaching on sex before marriage. The survey was conducted among 33,000 young people across the UK.

Seminar topic

In the light of the information outlined in this paragraph:

How important is it that young people follow the guidance of their religious leaders on sexual matters?

Contraception

One of the explanations given for the rise in sex before marriage among young people, as we have already seen, is the easy availability of contraception. Young people can now have sexual intercourse, using contraceptive devices with appropriate medical or professional advice, without fear of resulting pregnancy. This raises a number of important ethical issues:

- For some religions, artificial contraception methods are in themselves immoral since they interfere with the natural purpose of the sexual act, namely, the procreation of children. For example, the Roman Catholic Church takes a very firm view on this matter and would reject the use of artificial contraceptive methods by husband and wife within marriage (see the Catholic Report, Humanae Vitae). It would certainly reject sex before marriage as unethical and sinful, and the use of artificial contraception then would, of course, be completely rejected.

- Other religious leaders reluctantly recognise that sex before marriage is inevitable among young people. And although they would condemn this and discourage it, they nevertheless believe that it is better to encourage the use of contraception than to risk the possibility of unwanted pregnancy, with all the medical and ethical issues it raises.

- The rise in the incidence of AIDS/HIV has deepened the moral dilemma for many. Casual sexual intercourse is one of the ways by which the virus is passed from person to person. Using condoms is one way of ensuring 'safe sex' (i.e. 'safe' from the danger of being infected by the virus). Their use should, therefore, be encouraged. On the other hand, to encourage their use as a way of preventing AIDS/HIV does not face up to the moral seriousness of condoning sex before marriage. In the African continent, for example, the AIDS/HIV pandemic is having devastating effects: very acute moral dilemmas are raised by the relationships between sexual promiscuity, the availability and use of contraception, and the affordability of preventative medication for people trapped in poverty.

Sex and marriage

As we have seen in chapter 7, most religions teach that sexual intercourse is ethically acceptable only within marriage and that sexual relationships outside marriage are immoral under all circumstances. However, there are signs that some religions recognise that young people do have sexual intercourse before marriage. There are religious leaders, therefore, who reluctantly accept this situation and are prepared to condone the inevitability of sex before marriage, provided it is between two people who have made a commitment to be married to one another.

During recent decades in Britain and, indeed, in Western society generally, fewer weddings have been solemnised in Christian churches and consequently there has been an increase in secular weddings - in Register Offices, hotels etc. At the same time, there has been an increase in the number of people who decide to live together as partners without getting married, and who give birth to children and bring them up within such a relationship. There is also an increase in the number of people who have lived together as partners in this way and have given birth to children and, at a later date, decide to be married. This trend raises difficult moral questions for Christian churches: should Christian churches (that believe that marriage is the only sacred bond for sexual relationships and the procreation of children) be prepared to solemnise marriage between two people who have lived together as sexual partners?

Tasks

Writing tasks	(a)	Explain the ethical issues raised by sex before marriage.
	(b)	'In a society such as Britain, where there is much greater sexual freedom than in the past, religious leaders should recognise that sex before marriage is inevitable and adapt their teaching accordingly.'
		Evaluate this view from the perspective of one major world religion.

Glossary

pandemic   a large scale disease epidemic affecting all or most of the population of a
                     nation, region or continent

Homosexuality

The nature of homosexuality

Homosexuality involves a sexual relationship between two people of the same sex. These relationships are often described as 'gay' or, in the case of relationships between two women, 'lesbian'. (Sexual relationships between people of different sexes are defined as heterosexual).

There is considerable debate about whether homosexuality is merely a lifestyle chosen by certain individuals or whether it has a biological or genetic origin. Some researchers have claimed that homosexual orientation is in place very early in life, perhaps before birth. Research seems also to indicate that about 10% of the population is homosexual, a proportion which remains the same across a range of different cultural, religious and moral contexts. Others have claimed that there is no evidence that there is a biological or genetic basis for homosexuality and that it is, therefore, a matter of personal choice rather than an unchangeable characteristic.

Homosexuality and the law

In November 2000, after a long debate in both houses, the UK Parliament passed a new law that lowered the age of homosexual consent (i.e. the age above which homosexual acts would be legally permitted between two consenting persons) from 18 years to 16 years. This means that homosexuals are now subject to the same age consent law as heterosexuals. There was a very strong lobby of religious leaders and groups that sought to oppose this development on ethical grounds, but also because it was felt that the new law could make young people increasingly vulnerable to sexual abuse.

Class discussion

'Since homosexuality is a matter of biological orientation rather than personal choice, there can be no ethical objection to same sex relationships between consenting adults.'

'Since homosexuality is unnatural, has no biological or genetic basis, and is entirely a matter of personal choice, it should not be permitted by law.'

Evaluate the ethical implications of these conflicting views.

Ethical issues

Homosexuality raises a number of inter-related ethical issues:

- if the primary purpose of sex is the procreation of children, then homosexual relationships would be contrary to this purpose and should, therefore, be regarded as unethical;

- on the other hand, if the main purpose of sex is to give physical expression to mutual feelings of affection and love, then it could be argued that same sex relationships are as ethically acceptable as sexual relationships between opposite sexes;

- biologically, there is compatibility between the male and female sex organs, which seems to suggest that sexual relationships between them are natural, whereas same sex relationships are unnatural, (and, therefore, ethically unacceptable);

- if homosexuality has a biological or genetic basis, and is not a matter of personal choice, on what grounds can society claim that homosexual relationships are unethical? Can society insist that those of homosexual orientation should be celibate (i.e. should refrain from sexual relationships)?

- on the other hand, if homosexuality is a matter of choosing a particular personal lifestyle, then is it morally acceptable to condone same sex relationships? Or should those concerned undertake an educational programme to change their lifestyle?

Task

Writing task	'The primary purpose of sex is the procreation of children. It is clear, therefore, that homosexual relationships are ethically unacceptable.' Evaluate this view from the perspective of one major world religion.

Religions and homosexuality

Traditionally, most religions that have considered the morality of homosexuality have condemned it as immoral and incompatible with religious teaching.

- Islam forbids gay and lesbian relationships.

- Buddhism regards homosexual relationships as 'unwise' or unnatural, commends self-control in all sexual relationships, but also recognises that religious, social and cultural contexts change, and that religious responses to homosexuality (and, of course, to other ethical issues) may well need to be revised in the light of such changes.

- Hindu and Sikh literary sources are generally silent on the issue of homosexuality, but homosexual practice would seem to be out of line with traditional views on sexual morality.

- Traditionally, Judaism has condemned homosexuality as immoral, largely on the basis of the prohibition in Leviticus (e.g. Leviticus 18: 22).

Task

Research/ Writing task	Use the Religion and Ethics pages on the BBC website (http://news.bbc.co.uk) to find information about the approaches of one major world religion to homosexuality:
	• summarise the main ethical principles of your chosen religion in relation to homosexuality;
	• discuss whether these principles are still valid today;
	• prepare a short article on this topic that could be included in a school magazine or similar publication.

The Christian response

As an example of the way in which one world religion approaches homosexuality, the following section focuses on Christian responses to the ethical issues raised by homosexuality.

Traditionally, Christians have condemned homosexuality on the grounds that it is

* contrary to scripture, and

* contrary to the Natural Law (which, it is claimed, demands that the only purpose of sexual acts is procreation).

For example, in a chapter that sets out a detailed code of sexual relations, God's people are commanded:

> 'You shall not lie with a male as with a woman; it is an abomination'
>
> Leviticus 18: 22

In his letter to the Corinthians Paul condemns homosexual acts in the same breath as he condemns other sexual sins and personal and criminal offences:

> 'Fornicators, idolaters, adulterers, male prostitutes, sodomites, thieves, the greedy, drunkards, revilers, robbers - none of these will inherit the kingdom of God.'
>
> I Corinthians 6: 9-10

On this basis, Christians have traditionally condemned those who practice homosexuality, although in more recent years some sympathy has been shown towards those who have 'a homosexual condition'. For example, the Catholic Catechism states clearly that,

'Basing itself on Sacred Scripture, which presents homosexual acts as acts of grave depravity, Tradition has always declared that "homosexual acts are intrinsically disordered." They are contrary to the Natural Law. They close the sexual act to the gift of life... Under no circumstances can they be approved... (Therefore), homosexual persons are called to chastity.'

The Catholic Catechism, para. 2357-8

New approaches

In recent years, however, some Christian leaders and scholars have been exploring alternative responses to homosexuality. One of the key issues in this exploration has been whether the traditional understanding of the Bible offers an adequate basis for condemning homosexuality in the way that the Christian tradition has done.

For example, Bishop John Spong of the Episcopal Church of the USA reminds us that the Bible was used - wrongly, he would claim - in the past to defend slavery, to oppose new ways of treating illnesses and, more recently, to prevent women from being ordained.[67] Those who held these views claimed that they were acting on the basis of the indisputable teaching of the Bible. However, Bishop Spong believes that the Bible cannot be used in this way and that, moreover, 'the Bible is an ambiguous document about specific sexual practices... A real knowledge of scripture does not issue in certainty.'[68]

Another Christian leader, Bishop Richard Holloway, of the Episcopal Church in Scotland, holds a similar view and calls on Christians to think again about using the Bible as a final authority on matters of sexual ethics, and especially on issues relating to homosexuality. 'Christians did this in relation to the morality of slavery, which would be condemned today by all Christians. It now needs to be done in relation to homosexuality.'[69]

If the views of these Christian leaders (and there are a great many people who share these views) are to be taken seriously, a different approach to the ethics of homosexuality becomes possible. For example, if the key ethical concept in the New Testament (especially in the teaching of Jesus) is love (God's love for human beings, reflected in the love of human beings for one another), then it could be argued that homosexuality is ethically acceptable from a Christian perspective. This is, of course, provided it is not casual and promiscuous but is the physical expression of genuine mutual affection and love between two people of the same sex, within a committed relationship and partnership.

Class discussion

Recent reports indicate that an increasing number of Christian clergy and ministers are prepared to offer a service of blessing for gay and lesbian couples who wish to affirm their partnership within a Christian act of worship. The Lesbian and Gay Christian Movement has welcomed this development as 'bold, prophetic and courageous'.

Discuss whether Christian churches should officially offer this service to lesbian and gay couples.

Changing attitudes to homosexuality

We have already noted on page 101 above that, in the UK, the legal position in relation to homosexual acts has changed in recent years. This change reflects great changes in social attitudes in the United Kingdom, especially among young people. Recent research by Professor J. Leslie Francis (see chapter 8)[70] has suggested that there is a wide range of views among young people within the various world religions in the UK.

For example, whereas overall 38% of young people felt homosexuality to be wrong, 55% of Muslim youth felt that homosexuality was wrong compared with 38% of Christian youth, 31% of Sikhs, 28% of Hindus and 24% of Jews. There was considerable variation among the Christian churches and denominations also. 71% of young Christians who are members of new or non-traditional churches (sometimes called Christian sects) believed that homosexuality was wrong, compared with 37% of Catholic youth, 34% of non-conformist youth and 34% of Anglican youth.

Seminar topic

In the light of the information outlined above:

(1) How would you explain

   (a) the different attitudes among young people within the various world religions to homosexuality;

   (b) the different attitudes to homosexuality among young people within various Christian churches and denominations, as compared to those of their religious leaders?

(2) Conduct a simple survey on sexual attitudes within your class, school or college and compare your findings with those of Professor Leslie Francis.

(3) Present the results of your survey using computer graphics.

Tasks

Writing tasks	(a)	Outline the main ethical issues raised by homosexuality.
	(b)	'Since the Bible presents homosexual acts as acts of grave depravity, homosexuality is fundamentally immoral.' 'Since homosexuality can be the physical expression of genuine mutual affection and love between two people of the same sex, religions should revise their moral codes to make homosexuality ethically acceptable.' Discuss which of these views is most valid in today's society.

Perspectives of individual world religions on sexual issues discussed in chapters 7-9 are considered in greater detail in chapters 7-9 of the Religions and Ethics Teachers' Handbook.

Buddhism and sexual ethics

Marriage and Adultery
To marry is to enter the life of a householder, usually through a civil contract. Unfaithfulness is in disharmony with the marriage bond.

Divorce
Normally accepted if it is seen as the best course of action for all concerned.

How does Buddhism understand sexual ethics?

Sex before Marriage
Sex before marriage is contrary to precepts. Friendships between people of different or same sex 'do not involve sexual relationships'.

Homosexuality
Self-control is the high moral path. Same sex relationships are 'unwise or unnatural'. Recognition that views change from context to context.

Christianity and sexual ethics

Marriage and Adultery
Marriage is ordained by God as part of created order. It's seen as a sacrament or covenant. Purpose: procreation, mutual love and affection. Adultery is immoral.

Divorce
Jesus forbade divorce except for unchastity (see Matthew 5) Churches have traditionally followed this teaching. Others recognise the effect of social change on moral attitudes.

How does Christianity understand sexual ethics?

Sex before Marriage
Traditionally, sexual intercourse is allowed only within the marriage bond. Recent social trends have led some to have a more open view but long-term commitment and love are key.

Homosexuality
Traditionally it is against same sex relations (see Leviticus and Corinthians). Recent thinking among some leaders and their members has led to some changed attitudes.

Hinduism and sexual ethics

Marriage and Adultery
Marriage is important for individuals and society and is seen as sacrament. The woman is transferred to her husband. Goals: Progeny, faithfulness and mutual support. Adultery is immoral.

Divorce
Divorce is fairly easy among lower class Hindus. Taking another wife is encouraged when there is no son. The practice usually disadvantages women.

How does Hinduism understand sexual ethics?

Sex before Marriage
Premarital chastity is very important, especially for women. There is strong pressure to control the senses before marriage. There is growing evidence that pre-marital sex is accepted if marriage follows.

Homosexuality
Hindu literary sources are silent on homosexuality. It appears to be out of line with traditional norms. It is a taboo topic.

Islam and sexual ethics

Marriage and Adultery
The norm for Muslims, marriage has a divine sanction. A mutual contract between husband and wife. Inter-faith marriage is discouraged. Should be permanent. More than one wife is allowed.

Divorce
There are grounds for divorce in the Qur'an, including failure to discharge marital duties and to live with each other in peace and compassion.

How does Islam understand sexual ethics?

Sex before Marriage
Sexual intercourse is seen as an act of worship. Sex outside marriage is prohibited.

Homosexuality
Gay and lesbian relationships are forbidden by Muslim law.

Judaism and sexual ethics

Marriage and Adultery
Marriage imitates the relationship of Adam and Eve. Men (but not women) are required to marry. It is desirable to have children and a duty upon men.

Divorce
Divorce is possible within the Jewish law by agreement of partners. Men are allowed to break the marriage contract; it is not as easy for women.

How does Judaism understand sexual ethics?

Sex before Marriage
Technically, sexual intercourse is a state of marriage and should be confined to those married. The letter of the law is lax but interpretation is strict.

Homosexuality
Homosexuality is a matter of practice, not identity or orientation. It is prohibited in, for example, Leviticus 18 and 20.

Sikhism and sexual ethics

Marriage and Adultery

There is a high regard for marriage. It fuses two souls into one so that they become inseparable. Monogamy is the norm, but there are exceptions. Lifelong commitment is expected.

Divorce

Divorce occurs increasingly. Reconciliation should always be sought. There is a stigma, especially for divorced women.

How does Sikhism understand sexual ethics?

Sex before Marriage

Traditionally, because Sikhs lived in extended families, premarital sex was unthinkable, impractical and indefensible.

Homosexuality

Sikhs have not written on this subject. The expectation is that everyone marries and has children - especially women.

Chapter 9

Glossary

chastity	sexual self control and discipline, refraining from sexual relationships and acts
ordained	this has two meanings: (a) 'ordained by God' usually means 'commanded by God'; for example, 'marriage is ordained by God'; (b) it can also mean 'set apart for ministry'; 'women being ordained', for example, refers to women being set apart by the Church as priests or ministers.
orientation	personal tendency towards particular attitudes, feelings or relationships

Moral Theories and Sexual Ethics

Aim

The aim of this chapter is to enable you to

* *recall the key principles of the three moral theories studied, namely, Natural Law, Utilitarianism and Situation Ethics;*

* *reflect again on some of the fundamental issues raised by the aspects of sexual ethics studied in previous chapters; and*

* *explore ways in which the ethical theories can be applied to these aspects of sexual ethics.*

Many people within our society would wish to reject any and all religion as a basis for sexual ethics (or, indeed, as a basis for any other aspect of ethics). So we need to ask: **Do any moral theories offer a sound basis for sexual ethics?**

This question will now be considered in relation to the three moral theories which have been outlined in earlier chapters, namely, Natural Law, Utilitarianism and Situation Ethics.

Natural Law

The main characteristics of Natural Law (chapter 2) are as follows:

* there is a purpose and design in the natural world;

* for believers it is rooted in God's divine purpose;

* the ultimate aim of human life is to fulfil this divine purpose;

* the goal of ethics or morality is to set out a framework for human behaviour that enables human beings to achieve this highest good.

Chapter 2 focused particularly on sexual ethics as an example of the way in which Natural Law can be applied to human behaviour. Traditionally, Natural Law - especially within the Christian context - claims that

* the purpose and highest aim of sexual relationships, especially sexual intercourse, is to procreate children;

* that purpose and aim can only be fulfilled between a man and a woman within marriage;

* any other form of sexual activity is contrary to the Natural Law and, therefore, morally unacceptable;

* consequently, sex before marriage, artificial contraception, adultery, and homosexuality are all regarded as immoral.

On this basis, Natural Law would regard as immoral all sexual activity that is outside the marriage relationship between a man and a woman. This has been the traditional understanding within Christian moral teaching.

On the other hand, it would be possible to argue that:

- heterosexual relationships and homosexual relationships alike spring from natural instincts rooted within the reality of human nature;

- sexual activity is a natural consequence of sexual attraction within such relationships;

- sexual activity by heterosexuals and homosexuals should, therefore, be regarded as morally acceptable;

- the primary condition would be that such sexual activity seeks not to exploit others, but to serve the greatest good by seeking the greatest happiness, and to celebrate and nurture love.

On this basis, it could be argued that Natural Law would regard as immoral only that sexual activity which exploits others and therefore fails to serve the highest good.

It should be recognised, however, that although this is a way of interpreting the basic philosophy of Natural Law, historically Natural Law has been seen as providing a theoretical framework for developing a universal Christian morality.

In both cases, Natural Law seeks to define the morality of sexual activity in terms of the activity itself, rather than in terms of its consequences for individuals or families. It seeks to develop universally applicable sexual ethics.

Task

Writing task	'Natural Law and religious teachings complement each other and provide clear ethical teaching for our contemporary society.' Evaluate this view in relation to sexual ethics.

Utilitarianism

The basis of Utilitarianism (chapter 3) is that human beings 'should aim in all situations where there is a moral choice, to act in such a way as to ensure the greatest happiness for the greatest number of people.'

Bentham suggested the hedonic calculus as a means of defining this happiness or pleasure. Mill offered a refinement of Bentham's theory by suggesting, among other things, a distinction between superior pleasures and inferior pleasures.

How could Utilitarianism be applied to sexual ethics? It would be necessary to ask a series of questions in order to develop a response to this basic question:

- Does the sexual activity envisaged lead to the greatest happiness?

- Whose greater happiness is served; who is caused greatest pain?

- Does the happiness or pain affect only the individuals directly concerned, or would it have an impact on a wider group within a family or community?

- Is the happiness or pain short-lived or long-lasting, superficial or intense?

- Would the sexual activity enrich or impoverish the lives of the two individuals concerned? In other words, to use Mill's criteria, would the sexual activity be ultimately good and beneficial? Would it serve our desire for truth and beauty, love and friendship?

So Utilitarianism does not ask whether an act is morally good in and of itself, but asks rather 'What would be the consequences of the act for the persons concerned and those around them?'

It does not seek to offer a universal law. Rather it offers ethical guidelines - in the form of key questions - by which judgements can be made about the moral consequences of a particular act within a particular context.

Task

Writing task	'The current increase in sexual promiscuity requires a code of sexual ethics that provides firm and clear guidelines for sexual conduct, especially for young people. A Utilitarian approach to sexual ethics cannot provide the necessary guidance.'
	Evaluate this view.

Situation Ethics

The main characteristics of Situation Ethics (chapter 4) are:

- the rejection of absolute moral rules or laws that should be applied in all situations;

- an insistence that there is only one principle for morality, namely, the law of love, which is the only absolute rule;

- consequently, in any particular situation, the right thing to do is what love demands.

Therefore, Situation Ethics is based on four working principles, namely:

- Pragmatism: the act under consideration must be likely to achieve its aims.

- Relativism: different circumstances require different responses.

- Positivism: in considering the morality of any act, a decision in favour of love is fundamental.

- Personalism: people rather than moral law must always come first.

How can this theory be applied to sexual ethics? A number of basic statements can be confidently made:

(i)   Situation Ethics cannot provide a universal sexual ethic that can be applied in every situation. Each situation must be judged within its own terms. Therefore, sexual activity that is morally acceptable in one situation may not be morally acceptable in another.

(ii) The key question to ask in relation to any sexual act is: Does it serve first and foremost the law of love? A sexual act is immoral if it does not serve the demands of the law of love.

(iii) People must come first and, therefore, only those acts are moral that put the interests of all the people in the situation first.

So Situation Ethics provides a framework for sexual ethics which seeks to apply, in every situation, the demands of the law of love rather than the codes of a universal law.

Task

Writing task	'Current attitudes towards sexual conduct are too concerned with immediate physical pleasures and fail to understand sexual activity as the ultimate fulfilment of loving relationships.' Examine whether Situation Ethics helps to counteract this trend.

Natural Law and sexual ethics

Sex before Marriage
- The primary purpose of sex is the procreation of children.
- Marriage was written into the design and purpose of the universe as the God-given relationship for the procreation and nurture of children.
- So the 'highest good' of sex can be found only in marriage.

Homosexuality
- Same-sex relationships are regarded as unethical because they are contrary to the purpose and design of the universe and therefore 'unnatural'.
- They are also unethical because they cannot by definition lead to the procreation of children and are, therefore, contrary to the purpose of sex.

What does Natural Law say about sexual ethics?

Adultery and Divorce
- Since sexual relationships are ethical only within marriage, adultery is always unethical, whether or not it is regarded as harmful to others.
- Although marriage is intended to be between one man and one woman, and is regarded as a life-long commitment, sometimes 'unchastity' on the part of one partner may be regarded as justifying divorce but not remarriage.

Utilitarianism and sexual ethics

Sex before Marriage
- On the basis of the principle of 'the greater happiness', sex before marriage could be ethical because it could lead to the happiness of those concerned, but unethical because it could cause unhappiness to others.
- On the basis of consequentialism, sex before marriage could be ethical (e.g. it leads to deeper love) or unethical if it leads to an unwanted child or if it leads to medical, social or economic hardship.

Homosexuality
Similar arguments could be deployed here:
- if the homosexual relationship leads to the greatest happiness of those concerned,
- if it does not lead to harm or hurt to other people,
- if it is between consenting adults, and
- if adequate precautions are being taken by both persons against any harmful consequences to them (e.g. HIV/AIDS), then homosexuality could be regarded as ethical.

What does Utilitarianism say about sexual ethics?

Adultery and Divorce
- 'The principle of greatest happiness' could point to the conclusion that adultery is moral if all concerned would be happier as a result; but this is an unlikely situation.
- The consequentialist argument could regard adultery as ethical, provided it did not cause anyone any harm.
- Divorce may be unethical if the greatest happiness (e.g. of children) is denied, but ethical if all parties are happier as a result.

Situation Ethics and sexual ethics

Sex before Marriage

Situation Ethics would ask: what does the absolute law of love require in this particular and unique situation? It would ask a number of questions:

- Is genuine love or sexual desire the motive?
- Is this a loving relationship or casual sex?
- Is giving expression to love causing injustice to others?
- Does this act of love also serve the good of others or does it harm others?

Homosexuality

The same questions would be asked of homosexuality. Answers might be that it is ethical if:

- the motive is genuine love and not sexual desire;
- there is mutual love and no exploitation;
- there is mutual commitment and responsibility within the relationship;
- love towards others (partners, children or other family members) is not undermined.

What does Situation Ethics say about sexual ethics?

Adultery and Divorce

Whether or not adultery would be regarded as ethical would depend on answers to similar questions. For example,

- Is the motive genuine love or desire?
- Would committing adultery harm others or destroy the love of others?
- Does it grow out of mutual commitment?

Similarly, divorce would be ethical only if it is the most loving response to a situation and does not cause others hurt, injustice or pain.

Glossary

complement	(note the spelling!) to go together; to support each other
universal Christian morality	a Christian ethic which should be accepted and followed throughout the worldwide Christian family

Material for the Synoptic Module (A2)

Throughout your study of Religion and Ethics your teacher will have been alerting you to the information that you should bear in mind for the Synoptic Module that will be assessed at the end of your study of A2.

The assessment for the Synoptic module requires you to write an essay under controlled conditions on a specified aspect of either Religious Authority, or Religious Experience, or Life, Death and Life after Death. This essay should draw on at least two areas of study, because you are required to be able to sustain a critical line of argument, which may involve comparing and contrasting different areas of study.

As well as having the required knowledge and understanding of one of the three areas identified for synoptic assessment, you will need to demonstrate some critical reflection and the ability to sustain a line of argument.

Religious Authority

The WJEC specification indicates that the following aspects are relevant to this topic:

- God as the source of and warrant for the moral beliefs of religious believers;

- the existence of moral feelings and beliefs as an authoritative argument for God's existence;

- challenges to the authority of moral absolutism;

- challenges to the authority of religious concepts of truth and morality;

- challenges to the place of moral conscience in determining attitudes and behaviour.

The specification also suggests that in preparation for the Synoptic Module you should reflect upon:

- the place of ethical theory and argument as sources of authority for ethics, including conscience, law and religious teaching.

As a first step, it would be helpful to try to define what is meant by the term 'religious authority' and to describe the way in which the nature of, and sources for, 'religious authority' varies from religion to religion. You might find it helpful to look again at the following sections of earlier chapters in this book, for material that would be relevant to these aspects of Religious Authority:

(i) **God as the source of, and warrant for, the moral beliefs of religious observers:** The sections in chapter 5 on 'Religious concepts and moral attitudes' will offer guidance on this aspect of the topic. You should also reflect on the way in which attitudes to sexual morality (as outlined in chapters 7 - 9) may be affected by belief in God. Remember that 'God as source of moral beliefs' and 'God as warrant for moral beliefs' will need to be explored.

(ii) **The existence of moral feelings and beliefs as an authoritative argument for God's existence**: This issue is not addressed directly in this book, but you may wish to reflect on the degree to which the existence of the moral feelings and beliefs described throughout these chapters are dependent upon belief in God. Do such moral feelings and beliefs in themselves point to the existence of God?

In a sense, these two issues are two aspects of the same argument: Is the existence of God essential as a warrant for moral beliefs? If this is the case, does the evident existence of moral beliefs point in an authoritative way to the existence of God?

(iii) **Challenges to the authority of moral absolutism:** Ask yourself: What are the main challenges to the authority of moral absolutism?

Chapters 1 - 4 explore this issue in relation to ethical theories, since the question of moral absolutism is a central concern in Natural Law, Utilitarianism and Situation Ethics. You will have realised that these ethical theories reach very different conclusions about 'the authority of moral absolutism'.

Chapter 5 also explores this issue in relation to the ethical precepts of the world religions. Look particularly at the sections on absolute rules, general principles and personal circumstances.

Chapters 7 - 9 touch on the question of moral absolutism in relation to sexual ethics.

(iv) **Challenges to the authority of religious concepts of truth and morality:** Ask yourself: What are the main challenges to the authority of religious concepts of truth and morality?

Chapter 3 on Utilitarianism sets out an ethical theory that was aimed specifically at providing a foundation for morality which did not depend on the existence of a transcendent being. Reflect on the degree to which Utilitarianism succeeds in its aim: does it offer confirmation of, or a challenge to, 'the authority of religious concepts of truth and morality'?

In studying your chosen section of chapter 5 on The Ethical Precepts of the World Religions, you should consider whether the scepticism about religious claims, which is evident in Western society today, challenges the moral teaching of those religions.

If scepticism about religious claims does challenge the moral authority of religion, then ask yourself whether there are alternative sources of authority for ethics. Logical Positivism (which is studied in the A2 Religion and Ethics module) raises these questions particularly sharply and concludes that ethical statements are, in fact, non-sensical. Is there a basis for ethics without religion?

(v) **Challenges to the place of moral conscience in determining attitudes and behaviour:** All the chapters in this book touch on the place of the individual conscience in relation to moral attitudes and behaviour. The following inter-related questions are among those you should think about:

What are the main challenges to the place of moral conscience? What is the place of the individual conscience in a religion that makes absolute claims in relation to ethical behaviour? How can a conflict between individual conscience and the teaching of a particular religion be resolved? Is the individual moral conscience in and of itself an adequate basis for morality? Is it possible to resolve conflicts between the moral consciences of individuals in a society in order to reach a consensus on an ethical issue? In a democratic society where the decisions of the majority prevail, should there be a place for the moral conscience of the minority?

(vi) **The place of ethical theory and argument as sources of authority for ethics, including ethical theory and argument, conscience, law and religious teaching:** This is a key question raised by chapters 2 - 4 on Natural Law, Utilitarianism and Situation Ethics respectively, and by chapter 6 on the relationships between religions and ethical theories. This issue raises one of the most fundamental questions for ethics: are ethical theories valid and adequate sources of ethical authority? Comments in chapters 2 - 4 on the strengths and weaknesses of the theories are particularly relevant here.

Religious experience

The WJEC specification indicates that the following aspects are relevant to this topic:

- the effects of experiencing Creation on ethical attitudes towards the environment;

- the effects of reading sacred writing on ethical attitudes towards the environment;

- the ethics of stimulating religious experiences such as conversion and a sense of awe and wonder;

- challenges to the belief that religious experience is essential for ethical behaviour.

The specification also suggests that in preparation for the Synoptic Module you should reflect upon:

- the role of religious experience in making ethical decisions.

As a first step, it would be helpful to try to define the nature of 'religious experience' and to describe what aspects of religion contribute to 'religious experience' (e.g. worship, meditation). You might find it helpful to look again at the following sections in earlier chapters in this book, for material that would be relevant to these aspects of religious experience:

(i) **The effects of experiencing Creation on ethical attitudes towards the environment:** Ethical attitudes towards the environment are not included in the Introduction to Religion and Ethics module (AS) but the following sections might be helpful:

- Chapter 2 on Natural Law looks at the place of an awareness of order and design in the universe as a basis for ethical decision making. How would Natural Law theory contribute to an environmental ethic for today - for example, does Natural Law encourage or discourage scientific enquiry into the environment, such as genetic engineering? Would it help in developing an ethical code that guides society on which scientific enquiry and research is morally acceptable and which is not?

- Chapter 5 on The Moral Precepts of World Religions examines the way in which some religions (such as Hinduism) see the close interconnections between human beings and the natural order. How does this concept of 'connectedness' affect ethical attitudes to the environment?

- Chapter 5 also explores the understanding of God as creator in some world religions (such as Judaism and Christianity). How does belief in, and meditation on, a Creator God influence ethical attitudes towards the creation?

(ii) **The effects of reading sacred writing on ethical attitudes towards the environment:** The sections on each of the world religions in chapter 5 explore the place of religious or sacred text in developing ethical principles. These sections do not specifically raise the issue of environmental ethics, but candidates may wish to find examples from the texts referred to in chapter 5 to discover the way in which they influence attitudes towards the environment. For example, Judaism and Christianity would emphasise, in this context, Biblical passages such as the creation stories in Genesis (Chapters 1 and 2), the covenant with Noah in Genesis (Chapter 8), the Book of Job, and many of the Psalms, such as Psalm 8, 65 and 104. What are the ethical implications of these texts?

(iii) **The ethics of stimulating religious experiences such as conversion and a sense of awe and wonder:** The chapters in this book do not examine this issue directly. Many of the descriptions of world religions in chapter 5 assume that religious experience (such as meditation on God or reading sacred texts) and a sense of awe and wonder (not necessarily in strictly religious terms) will have ethical consequences. The morality of that natural process is not being questioned.

However, some religions see themselves as 'proselytising' religions, that is, they seek to convert people who either belong to other religions or have no religious attachment at all. Occasionally, considerable pressure is used to produce such a converting religious experience.

What are the motivations for such efforts at conversion? Is conversion to one's own religion a goal that justifies employing any means? Can conversion be justified at any cost? On what grounds can decisions about the ethics of such religious pressure be made? Some religions, such as Sikhism, describe themselves as non-proselytising religions and teach that all faiths are one and worship the one God. Does a morality that declares that all people and all religions are one and equal raise other, equally difficult, questions? For example, does refusing to be involved in converting others mean that religious truth is in the end sacrificed — that ultimate truth does not matter?

(iv) **Challenges to the belief that religious experience is essential for ethical behaviour:** Ask yourself: what are the challenges to the belief that religious experience is essential for ethical behaviour? Your answers might include the effects of an increasingly secular society and the rise of materialism, the diminishing importance of religious worship, developments in science.

Aspects of this issue were explored above in relation to 'religious authority'. Much of what was said then is valid also in relation to this issue. But other factors also need to be explored here. For example, are an experience of God, participation in religious worship or meditation, a pattern of personal or communal spirituality, belonging to a religious community, or study/reflection on sacred texts essential for ethical behaviour? Clearly, these practices would have an influence on ethical behaviour, but the question being posed is: can there be ethical behaviour without such experience? This brings us back to the question that we have considered already, namely, can there be a basis for ethics without religion?

Life, death and life after death

In relation to this topic, the WJEC specification highlights:

- concepts of "the sanctity of life" and "the quality of life", with particular reference to euthanasia and suicide;

- the impact of beliefs about life, death and life after death on ethical behaviour.

Generally, these issues will be studied in the Religion and Ethics option at A2 level and do not receive any detailed treatment in this book. The following are among the issues that need to be considered:

(i) **Concepts of "the sanctity of life" and "the quality of life", with particular reference to euthanasia and suicide:**

- what is the basis of the concept of 'the sanctity of life'? Is it possible to have an understanding of this concept without a religious basis?

- am I bound by the concept of the sanctity of my own life? You may not take my life without being accused of committing murder, but does the same principle hold when it is a matter of my taking my own life? On what basis would an ethical distinction be made?

- is the principle of 'the sanctity of life' an absolute principle (i.e. human life must be protected at all costs and under all circumstances), or are there situations in which it is justifiable to sacrifice human life for the sake of a greater good e.g. in a situation of war?

- when does 'the sanctity of life' come into play: does life in this sense begin at conception or at birth? Therefore, is abortion the taking of a human life and the betrayal of 'the sanctity of life'?

- similarly, does 'the sanctity of life' mean that human life must always be preserved even in extreme pain or illness or when there is no likelihood of recovery from deep unconsciousness?

- here, the concept of 'the quality of life' comes into play: how is the concept of 'the quality of life' evaluated and defined? What is its moral or ethical meaning? Do I have quality of life only when I am conscious of my own life experience, relationships etc. or can I have quality of life even if I have no memory left or any consciousness of what is happening to me or around me?

(ii) **The impact of beliefs about life, death and life after death on ethical behaviour:** Chapter 5 on The Ethical Precepts of World Religions touches on some of these issues, including:

- the relationship between belief in God or gods, the meaning of life and moral behaviour e.g. the concepts of karma, laksanas (the three marks of existence) and the Four Noble Truths in Buddhism;

- the relationship between life, death, life after death and reincarnation and enlightenment in Hinduism;

- the concept of connectedness in Hinduism;

- the concepts of reward and punishment, paradise/heaven and hell in some religions (such as some strands of Christianity and Islam) as motivations for a moral life.

Glossary

hell	a state of eternal damnation which some religions believe to be the punishment of those who are unbelievers or have disobeyed God's will
materialism	a way of life which is based on acquiring material possessions rather than on spiritual values, often rooted in a belief that the physical, material world is all there is
paradise/heaven	a state of eternal life which some religions believe to be the reward of the faithful after death
proselytising religions	religions which set out to convert people from other religions to their own
synoptic	in this context, taking an overall view of the material studied in at least two modules and making connections between them, in order to discuss a particular theme from various perspectives
warrant	guarantee

References

[1] Elford, R. John, *The Ethics of Uncertainty*, One World, 2000.

[2] In an unpublished document.

[3] Mel Thompson, *Ethical Theory*, Hodder and Stoughton, 1999, p.60.

[4] Aristotle, *Nichomachean Ethics*, Trans. J.A.K. Thomson, Penguin, 1976, p.64.

[5] Vardy and Grosch, p.132.

[6] Thompson, pp.75ff.

[7] ibid, p.76.

[8] Vardy, P. and Grosch, P., *The Puzzle of Ethics*, Fount, 1999, p.69.

[9] Mel Thompson, *Teach yourself Ethics*, Hodder and Stoughton, 2003, p.71.

[10] John Stuart Mill, *Utilitarianism: Essays on Ethics, Religion and Society*, ed. Robson, Priestley and Dryer, Toronto, 1969, p.214.

[11] Thompson (1999), pp.79ff.

[12] ibid, p.81.

[13] Quoted in Vardy and Grosch, p.123.

[14] Thompson (1999), p.115.

[15] Vardy and Grosch, pp.125ff.

[16] ibid, p.126.

[17] Thompson (1999), p.117.

[18] For fuller information on Buddhism, students are directed to *Buddhism for AS students* by Wendy Dossett, in the present series and to other accounts listed in the bibliography.

[19] ibid Chapters 3 and 4, upon which this summary is based.

[20] Stewart MacFarlane in *Making Moral Decisions*, ed. Jean Holm and John Bowker, Continuum, 1994, p.17.

[21] Dosset, p.32.

[22] Morgan, P. and Lawton, C. (eds.), in *Ethical Issues in Six Religious Traditions*, Edinburgh University Press, 1996, pp.74ff.

[23] ibid, p.58

[24] Richard Holloway, *Godless Morality: Keeping Religion Out of Ethics*, Canongate, Edinburgh, 1999, pp.80ff.

[25] Shannon, T., in Morgan and Lawton, p.201.

[26] ibid, p.176.

[27] Davies, D., in Holm and Bowker, p.60.

[28] Thompson (2003), p.156.

[29] This section depends heavily upon the essay on 'Indian Ethics' by Pursottama Bilimoria, in *A Companion to Ethics*, Singer (ed.), Blackwells, 1993.

[30] ibid, p.45.

[31] ibid, p.48.

[32] Quoted in ibid, p.50.

[33] Quoted by Werner Menski in Morgan and Lawton, p.5.

[34] Flood, Gavin D., in Holm and Bowker, p.68.

[35] Werner Menski in Morgan and Lawton, p.2.

[36] *The Oxford Dictionary of World Religions*, J. Bowker (ed.), OUP, 1997, p.432.

[37] ibid, p.432.

[38] Menski, p.6.

[39] Flood, p.72.

[40] Menski, p.4.

[41] Bilimoria, p.46.

[42] Flood, p.92.

[43] Thompson (2003), p.159.

[44] Outline based on ibid, pp. 159-60.

[45] Flood, p.71.

[46] ibid, p.72.

[47] ibid, p.81.

[48] ibid, p.82.

[49] ibid, pp.70ff.

[50] Menski, p.5.

[51] Morgan and Lawton.

[52] Statement by Rabbi Kassel Abelson, 1985, quoted in Cohn-Sherbok, L. and D., *Judaism*, Oneworld, 1997.

[53] ibid.

[54] Norman Solomon in Holm and Bowker.

[55] Flood.

[56] Indarjit Singh in Holm and Bowker.

[57] ibid.

[58] Quoted in Morgan and Lawton.

[59] ibid, p.58.

[60] Stewart MacFarlane in Holm and Bowker.

[61] ibid.

[62] Pope, Stephen J., 'Natural Law and Christian Ethics' in *A Cambridge Companion to Christian Ethics*, CUP, 2001.

[63] Spong, J.S., *Why Christianity must change or die*, Harper, San Francisco, 1998, p.159.

[64] ibid, p.166.

[65] Bilimoria, p.46.

[66] From a report in the *Western Mail*, 14 March 2001.

[67] Spong, pp.156ff.

[68] ibid, p.158.

[69] Holloway, pp.80ff.

[70] *Western Mail*.

Bibliography

Bowker, J., *The Oxford Dictionary of World Religions*, OUP, 1997

Cohn-Sherbok, L., and D., *Judaism: A Short Introduction*, Oneworld, 1997

Cook, D., *The Moral Maze*, SPCK, 1983

Holm, J., and Bowker J., (eds.), *Making Moral Decisions*, Continuum, 1994

Jenkins, J., *Ethics and Religion*, Heinemann, 1999

Morgan P., and Lawton, C., (eds.), *Ethical Issues in Six Religious Traditions*, Edinburgh, 1996

Thompson, M., *Teach Yourself Ethics*, Hodder and Stoughton, 2003

Vardy, P., and Grosch, P., *The Puzzle of Ethics*, Fount, 1994 and 1999